Secrets of Poser® Experts:
Tips, Techniques, and Insights for Users of All Abilities— The e frontier Official Guide

Daryl Wise and Jesse DeRooy

THOMSON

COURSE TECHNOLOGY

Professional ■ Technical ■ Reference

© 2007 Thomson Course Technology, a division of Thomson Learning Inc. All rights reserved. No part of this book may be reproduced or transmitted in any form or by any means, electronic or mechanical, including photocopying, recording, or by any information storage or retrieval system without written permission from Thomson Course Technology PTR, except for the inclusion of brief quotations in a review.

The Thomson Course Technology PTR logo and related trade dress are trademarks of Thomson Course Technology, a division of Thomson Learning Inc., and may not be used without written permission.

Poser is a registered trademark of e frontier. Photoshop is a registered trademark of Adobe Systems Incorporated. Bryce is a trademark of DAZ 3D. Painter is a registered trademark of Corel Corporation. 3ds Max is a registered trademark of Autodesk, Inc. All other trademarks are the property of their respective owners.

Important: Thomson Course Technology PTR cannot provide software support. Please contact the appropriate software manufacturer's technical support line or Web site for assistance.

Thomson Course Technology PTR and the authors have attempted throughout this book to distinguish proprietary trademarks from descriptive terms by following the capitalization style used by the manufacturer.

Information contained in this book has been obtained by Thomson Course Technology PTR from sources believed to be reliable. However, because of the possibility of human or mechanical error by our sources, Thomson Course Technology PTR, or others, the Publisher does not guarantee the accuracy, adequacy, or completeness of any information and is not responsible for any errors or omissions or the results obtained from use of such information. Readers should be particularly aware of the fact that the Internet is an ever-changing entity. Some facts may have changed since this book went to press.

Educational facilities, companies, and organizations interested in multiple copies or licensing of this book should contact the Publisher for quantity discount information. Training manuals, CD-ROMs, and portions of this book are also available individually or can be tailored for specific needs.

ISBN-10: 1-59863-263-9

ISBN-13: 978-1-59863-263-7

Library of Congress Catalog Card Number: 2006904398

Printed in the United States of America

07 08 09 10 11 BU 10 9 8 7 6 5 4 3 2 1

THOMSON

COURSE TECHNOLOGY

Professional ■ Technical ■ Reference

Thomson Course Technology PTR,
a division of Thomson Learning Inc.
25 Thomson Place
Boston, MA 02210
http://www.courseptr.com

**Publisher and General Manager,
Thomson Course Technology PTR:**
Stacy L. Hiquet

Associate Director of Marketing:
Sarah O'Donnell

Manager of Editorial Services:
Heather Talbot

Marketing Manager:
Heather Hurley

Acquisitions Editor:
Megan Belanger

Marketing Coordinator:
Adena Flitt

Development Editor:
Karen A. Gill

Project/Copy Editor:
Karen A. Gill

Technical Reviewer:
Steve Rathmann

PTR Editorial Services Coordinator:
Erin Johnson

Interior Layout:
Shawn Morningstar

Cover Designer:
Mike Tanamachi

DVD-ROM Producer:
Brandon Penticuff

Indexer:
Katherine Stimson

Proofreader:
Gene Redding

I can still see myself jumping up and down on a bed when I came up with the idea for software to provide a digital mannequin for artists. That was in 1989, when I was a computer graphics technical director by day and a frustrated cartoonist by night. I needed something to help me to visualize characters in pose and in perspective. Physical mannequins proved to be toys more than useful aids. My attempts to build my own mannequin from tubing and plumbing parts were fruitless. And the 3D software at the time was too complex and unwieldy.

So I started on an experiment to see if I could make something that was easier to use. My long-term goal was to help myself, and, if I could someday recover $10,000 for my efforts, I would be thrilled.

I never imagined that what I started would still be going strong into the next millennium and that more than a million people would use the software to unleash their creativity. I am still waiting to create a comic strip using the tool, but many others have—and that has been the rewarding thing. There have been stories of 30-something policemen and landscapers finding their true calling with Poser and landing creative roles with Marvel and DC comics. There are ex-Manson family prisoners rehabilitating with Poser. There are young children discovering how to put pictures to their thoughts. There are movies being previsualized using Poser. There are sculptures designed with it, advertisements created with it, and clothes designed with it. There are talented modelers making livings providing clothing, characters, and animals for the other Poser artists. There are "adults" creating images that are probably wonderful, but I don't need to see. There are forums and user groups that have spawned friendships, arguments, rivalries, hatreds, marriages, and thousands and thousands of incredible images.

With everything that Poser can now do—from motion capture playback to photo and non-photo-realistic rendering—what more can we dream for in the future? Well, maybe having more than one level of undo some day would be nice…

Larry Weinberg, Creator of Poser

Daryl Wise Acknowledgments

I would like to acknowledge the individuals who helped make this book possible. First, I would sincerely like to thank all the creative, passionate, and talented artists who have participated in this book. Special thanks to David Ho, Scott Thigpen, Fabrice Delage, and Brian Jon Haberlin for the cover images. I also want to thank all artists for making the world a better place to live.

Thanks, too, to my friend and book partner, Jesse DeRooy, for working with me while we put the book together. She worked closely with the editors on the details of the book and kept the book on track. She balanced her new family life while working long hours at the computer screen. Her creative eye gave this book a nice look and feel.

Thanks to Larry Weinberg for making a killer app! I worked at Fractal Design with Larry on the original Poser rollout. I have seen so much fabulous Poser artwork and know how Poser is used as a work tool for the creative professional and for the hobbyist. I am such a lucky guy to be part of this community!

Thank you to my friends at e frontier and everyone who works on Poser for the company. They are a good bunch who is committed to the company and to Poser. Thanks to Uli Klumpp, who leads the Poser engineering team and is the former Poser product manager. He has a huge responsibility and has expertly guided the Poser ship through the channels and rough seas, making Poser the successful software that it is.

And last, but not least, I want to thank the team that we worked with at Thomson for allowing us to write this book and for their encouragement throughout the book-writing process. Thanks to Acquisitions Editor Megan Belanger, who was so cool and easy to work with, Project Editor Karen Gill, who kept the project on course and made sure every detail was accounted for, and Tech Editor Steve "Rat" Rathmann, whose *complete* knowledge of Poser was essential for making sure all facts and technical portions of the book were correct. Steve and I worked together at Fractal Design and go "way back." Finally, thanks to Brandon Penticuff, who created the DVD, and Poser book author Kelly Murdock, who gave us the glossary that we used.

Jesse DeRooy Acknowledgments

I would like to thank Daryl Wise for inviting me to co-author this book with him. He has his finger on the pulse of art in the 3D community, and he knew how great this book would be from the beginning. I have learned so much from working with him. I am grateful that Daryl and I were able to bring our vision, experience, and expertise together to create something special: a direct connection to the artists who inspire us. I feel so lucky to have been able to work with the artists to compile this book of their secrets. They clearly demonstrate why creative people should have Poser in their digital production toolbox.

I would like to thank Steve Rathmann for all his great technical supervision of the artists' tips, techniques, and insights. Thank you especially to Karen Gill, without whom this book would be an unintelligible mess and because of whom I think that we have created something anyone can understand. Thank you Megan Belanger for being available to answer all the questions, and to the rest of the production crew at Thomson Course Technology, thanks for turning this book around so fast. Thanks also to Laena for taking a picture of Daryl and me.

To my family and friends: Thank you for giving me all the support that I needed to write this book. I couldn't have done it without you! I would also like to thank Larry Goldfarb, Ph.D., for helping to refine the interview questions that addressed the mechanics of posture, gesture, and expression. Thanks to Alice Palacio for making sure my posture was good while sitting at the computer, and to Chris for making me laugh and take breaks. Finally, I would like to thank my precious son, Preston, who during the time this book was written learned to walk. Preston, you're the joy of my life.

CHAPTER 1: David Ho

CHAPTER 2: Carina Dumais

CHAPTER 5: Daniel Scott Gabriel Murray

CHAPTER 6: Les Garner

CHAPTER 9: Tony Luke

CHAPTER 10: Gabriel Sabloff

CHAPTER 13: Mike Campau

CHAPTER 14: Scott Thigpen

Daryl Wise has worked as an independent public relations and marketing contractor for clients including e frontier (formerly Curious Labs), the artist Peter Max, Macworld Expos, Seybold Seminars, Gluon, Hewlett-Packard, Hewlett-Packard, Canada, Markzware, Bill Graham Presents, MTV, O'Neill, Inc., Rogers and Cowan Public Relations, Shandwick Convergence Public Relations, The Sea Otter Classic cycling event, The City of Watsonville, Laguna Seca Raceway, LatinReps, Meals on Wheels of Santa Cruz County, and the Catalyst and Palookaville nightclubs. Daryl wrote the book *Secrets of Award-Winning Digital Artists* and was the director of the Santa Cruz Digital Arts Festival for three years. He has moderated or participated in panel discussions at The Deviant Art Summit, Macworld Expo, and Seybold Seminars.

Jesse DeRooy graduated with a degree in applied interactive media (a degree she created for herself) from the University of California, Santa Cruz. She is an award-winning radio editor and independent filmmaker. She specializes in representing artists and their works to larger audiences through all forms of media. She lives and works in Santa Cruz, California with her partner Chris and son Preston.

Daryl and Jesse.

What You'll Find in This Book

When we were deciding on the overall concept for the book, we agreed that we wanted to give readers a feeling as if they were communicating with the artist, where they could ask questions and see detailed, step-by-step techniques. We also wanted to include incredible artwork and a DVD packed full of art galleries, videos, movies, tutorials, links, and content—all relating to Poser.

Who This Book Is For

This book offers *all* Poser and other graphic software users—from beginner to pro—a way to learn from Poser experts. This book was created to help readers understand Poser better. Although the book has in-depth technical information that is useful for the professional graphic designer or expert Poser artist, it also has simple step-by-step techniques and information that will be useful for hobbyists and novices. Poser software has been on the market for more than 10 years, and some of the experts featured in this book have been using it since it first became available. They really are experts!

How This Book Is Organized

This book is about the artists featured in this book, who we call "Poser experts." Each Poser expert wrote a chapter that details professional background, techniques, insights, and resources. Most also include a gallery highlighting some of their work. This book is organized into sections according to the expert's area of Poser expertise, such as illustration, content creation, comic, Web, motion graphics, photo-realism, and sci-fi/fantasy.

What's on the DVD

On the DVD-ROM included with this book, you will find many items submitted by the Poser experts, e frontier, and Content Paradise that we thought you would find useful and enjoyable. The "On the DVD" section toward the end of each chapter tells what is in that artist's folder.

The Poser experts featured in this book have a designated button on the DVD where you can access their art gallery, movies, videos, tutorials, links to their favorite Web sites, and free content. If you want to make the art gallery slideshow larger, increase your monitor resolution.

Please remember that the artwork, videos, movies, content, and tutorials are the property of the artists and cannot be reproduced without their permission. e frontier (maker of Poser) and Content Paradise (an e frontier company) supplied a demo version of Poser 6, the 3D human figure Koji 1.0, and the "Swap Pack" of bugs and swamp creatures. You can use the free content included for noncommercial use unless specified or by consent.

Note: Addition to the Koji 1 Read Me file: The Face room compatibility is *not* in development at this time as stated in the Read Me file.

How to Contact Us

Writing this book has been an enjoyable experience for us.
We hope that you will learn a great deal from it and that
it encourages you to become a Poser expert. We invite
you to e-mail us with any comments or thoughts.

All the best,

Daryl and Jesse
Poserbook@surfnetusa.com

DAVID HO

About the Artist

David has a bachelor's of art in sociology from UC Berkeley and a bachelor's of art in art history with a minor in fine arts from San Jose State University. David has been creating digital art for almost 15 years. His works have been accepted into numerous competitions, including the San Francisco Society of Illustrators, Step by Step Graphics Illustration, the Macworld Expo Digital Art Contest, and the Seybold Digital Art Gallery. David has also been featured in numerous publications, including *EFX Art and Design*, *Computer Arts*, and *Digital Photo User*.

David's clients have included the *Chicago Tribune*, Ziff Davis, Interscope Records, Sony Music, and the NRA. He has published an art book titled *Shadow Maker: The Digital Art of David Ho*.

Artist's Statement

I've always believed that art's purpose is to serve as an outlet for my thoughts, feelings, and expressions. Without Poser, I definitely would not be the artist I am today. Poser's wireframe and its ability to bring in other wireframe figures from places like daz3d.com are invaluable. No other software can create human figure gestures like Poser.

Influences

I've created art for so long that it's become a habit. Creating art makes me feel productive in this world. During different stages of my career, I've learned to admire different artists. When I first started out, I loved the works of Michael Whelan, Michael Parkes, and H. R. Giger; then the works of John Jude Palencar, Odd Nerdrum, Cam de Leon, and Mark Ryden started growing on me. I still love the works of these artists, but today I find myself looking at traditional Chinese paintings quite a bit.

Techniques

The Creative Process

I always create my dominant subject matter in Poser. I use Poser when I create figures, and most of my works are figurative. I work in grayscale first to concentrate on certain elements, such as lighting, composition, form, and texture. After I'm satisfied with the illustration, I convert the entire file into an RGB file and then start coloring each element in each layer.

Step-by-Step Tutorial: How to Create "Block Figures"

My series of block figures deals with themes on the disintegration and integration of man. The human form is portrayed within a series of blocks.

It took me roughly 6 months to nail down this technique, and I've never shared it with anyone until now. Creating this effect requires some skills in Photoshop and Poser and some textures that can be created digitally, traditionally, or from a digital camera.

I'll demonstrate this technique with the artwork "Letting Go." See Figure 1.12. To start out with, it's usually easier to work on this style with a close-up of a figure (as opposed to showing the entire figure).

1. Beginning with Figure 1.1, the pose is quite standard. It's always easier to create this "block" artwork when the figure is close-up. For the lighting, I use a single-source light. For the background, I pick a color that's entirely different from the figure. Later on, I'll select the figure separately from the background. I render the figure over black in Poser *without* texturing it. For this technique, I will add my own texture on top of the figure in Photoshop.

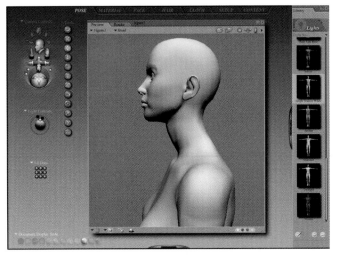

Figure 1.1 Close-up of stock figure.

TIP

If you're an artist who is just starting out with Poser, begin with more static poses. Users who aren't too familiar with Poser often end up trying to create figures in dramatic gestures, but those usually appear unconvincing.

2. After rendering the figure, I set the Document Display Style to Hidden Line. See Figure 1.2. Again, the color of the wireframe is drastically different from the background color. Output a high-resolution wireframe/hidden line view render of the figure. (See Note.)

NOTE

Depending on what version of Poser you are using, either output a high-resolution wireframe/hidden line view (Poser 5, 6, 7), or capture the screen if you are working with an older version. (On the Mac, press ⌘+Shift+3. For Windows, use the Print Scrn key.)

3. Using Photoshop, I open the Poser screenshot or high-resolution render and go to Select, Color Range and pick the background color. See Figure 1.3.

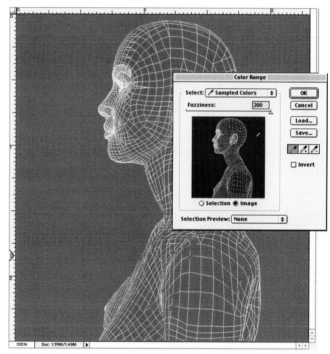

Figure 1.3 Select the background color in Photoshop.

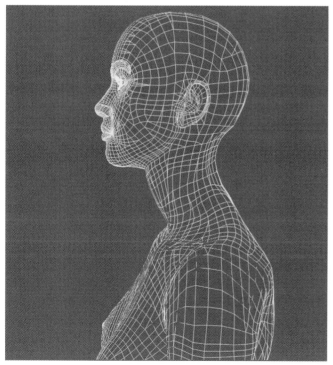

Figure 1.2 View Hidden Line and use contrasting line color.

4. Then I delete the background color so that only the image of the wireframe remains. See Figure 1.4.

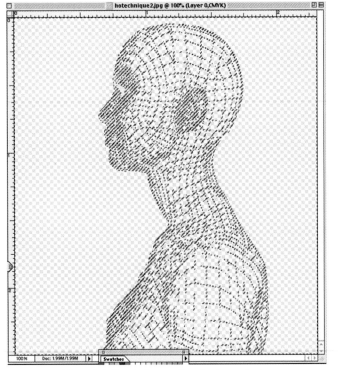

Figure 1.4 The wireframe with no background color.

5. Next, I open the rendered Poser file with a black background in Photoshop. Notice in Figure 1.5 that the file is still in grayscale at this point. For this technique, I do not convert to RGB or color the image until later.

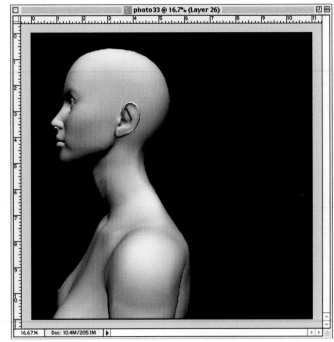

Figure 1.5 Open the rendered Poser file in Photoshop.

6. Now I bring in the previous wireframe file, color it black, copy it, and paste it onto the new file. Using the Scale tool, I adjust it so that the wireframe is the same size as the rendered figure. See Figure 1.6.

7. Notice in Figure 1.7 that the wireframe doesn't look all that great because it's been enlarged. Steps 8–12 show how I improve the look of the wireframe.

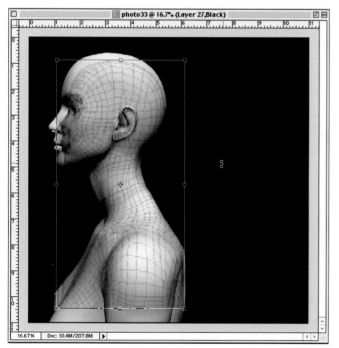

Figure 1.6 Add the block layer.

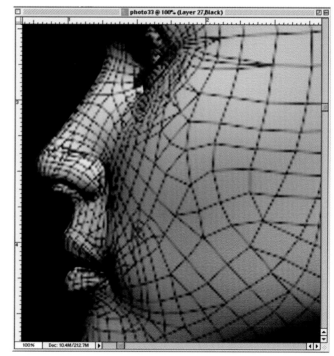

Figure 1.7 The enlarged wireframe.

TIP

Photoshop works great with Poser. I always create hair in Photoshop. Also, any 3D program has areas you need to clean up. Photoshop is effective at managing those touch-ups.

8. In Figure 1.8, I apply the Gaussian Blur filter to the wireframe (Filter, Blur, Gaussian Blur).

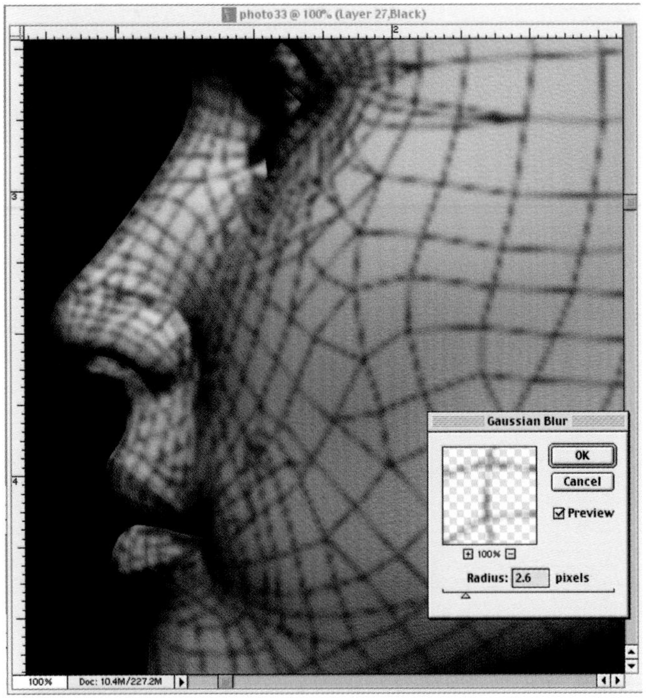

9. I go to Filter, Other, Maximum to sharpen the wireframe. If it appears a little light, I might want to duplicate the layer. See Figure 1.9.

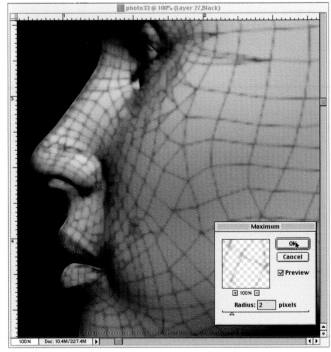

Figure 1.8 Apply the Gaussian Blur filter.

Figure 1.9 Duplicate the layer to darken it.

10. Figure 1.10 shows both of the rock textures I used in this piece. I don't think that any one texture is particularly better than another. The only manipulation that I did on the textures was probably adjusting the brightness and contrast. I place these two different textures in Overlay mode on top of the file.

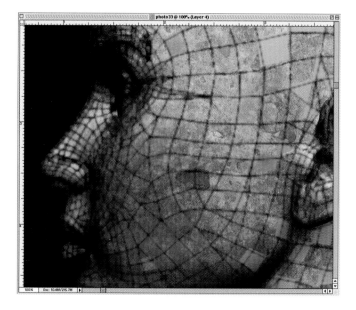

Figure 1.10 These rocks were scanned to create realistic overlay textures.

11. In Figure 1.11, I duplicate the wireframe and then color it white. I move the entire white frame a little and erase certain areas where the shadows were erased.

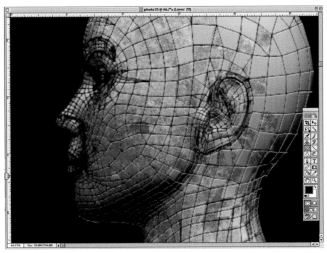

Figure 1.11 Offset the wireframe layer to give the illusion of depth.

12. In a nutshell, that's how I create the block feel. After I'm satisfied with the file, I convert it to RGB and color each layer individually. See Figure 1.12, which is the final image. I created the blocks in Bryce and then duplicated and rotated them.

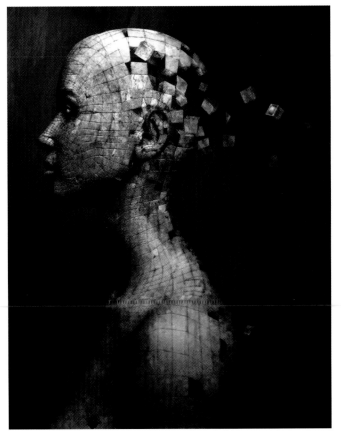

Figure 1.12 "Letting Go" final image.

ILLUSTRATION/SCI-FI FANTASY

Insights

Lighting

I love dramatic lighting. That's why I use the simple "single source light" so much in my figures. Every once in a while, I add a spotlight to add a more dramatic *chiaroscuro* effect. *Chiaroscuro* (Italian for light-dark) is a fine art technique that uses bold contrast between light and dark, which gives the illusion of more depth. In addition to creating more depth, shadows can help to hide the imperfections of the Poser figures. Sometimes I use the stock lighting scenes.

Content

The most important stock content for me is the hand gestures because they are a pain to adjust. Moving each joint and finger gets tedious. Having stock content really helps to eliminate the hassle. I find the best stock content at daz3d.com.

Posing Figures

Posing takes patience and lots of coffee. Getting the exact gesture, pose, or expression is the most challenging part of working with Poser. The hardest gestures are the action-oriented ones because of the complex way our bodies and muscles twist, expand, and contract. I like developing static poses to create a surreal, strange, and quiet mood. I also enjoy creating static facial expressions. While I'm creating the figure, I usually add a low-resolution image of the background in Poser so that adjusting the perspective and lighting of the figure is simpler. I usually bring all the files back into Photoshop to fit them together.

Memory Dots

Using Memory Dots is helpful. This feature remembers a certain pose after you click it. Memory Dots can temporarily save up to nine poses, camera angles, and user interface layouts. They are in the Poser workspace by default. You can access them by choosing Window, Memory Dots. Figure 1.13 shows Memory Dots.

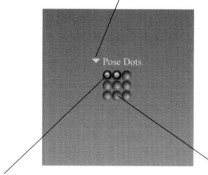

Use pop-up to choose camera, UI, or pose dots

Click empty dot to save   Click saved dot to recall

Figure 1.13 Memory Dots.

Q&A

What do you wish someone had told you when you first started with Poser?

I wish someone had told me the great leaps Poser would take. I remember using Poser 1. Boy, now that I think back, those figures were quite archaic.

Where do you think computer-generated imagery will be 5–10 years from now?

I think computer-generated imagery will take a turn toward a more abstract and expressionistic style. It's currently at a point where it's *so* realistic. After a while, people will consciously move away from realism and find their own style. It's similar to traditional arts, where hints of modern art came into play with the advent of Impressionism. In Impressionism, artists made a conscious effort not to make refined and realistic art.

DAVID HO

What do you think will be most significant in CGI 5–10 years from now?

I think it will be the infinite possibility of outputting hard copies. Now anyone can output his works on paper with the abundant supply of various printers out there. Maybe, just maybe, someone will invent some kind of sculpture outputting device where the artist can one day output his wireframe to sculpture at a reasonable cost.

Resources

On the DVD

- Three desktop wallpapers
- Artist Gallery

Links

- http://www.daz3d.com
- http://www.audrey-kawasaki.com/
- http://www.danielmartindiaz.com/
- http://www.happypencil.com/
- http://www.chrismarspublishing.com/
- http://www.nerdrum.com/
- http://www.stephenkasner.com/

DAVID HO

Studio

Software: Poser, Photoshop, Bryce, Illustrator
Hardware: Mac G5

Contact

David Ho ▪ ho@davidho.com ▪ http://www.davidho.com

Gallery

"Looking Inward."

"The Difference."

DAVID HO

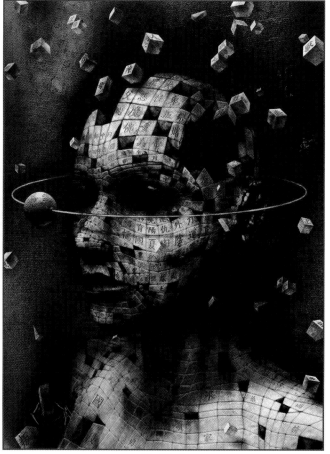

"The Way."

"World Order."

CARINA DUMAIS

About the Artist

Carina Dumais is a Dutch/Indonesian woman working as an expressive artist, illustrator, and entrepreneur. After studying at the Gerrit Rietveld Academy for visual arts in Amsterdam, she worked with traditional materials such as oil paint, red ochre, textile, and objects from nature. Her works have been purchased by art collectors in The Netherlands, Florida, and Greece, among them financial institutions and individuals.

After studying at the Graphic Media Institute, also situated in Amsterdam, Carina started using new media, especially computer software such as Poser and Photoshop. She now uses these tools to create visual art, design, artwork, and illustrations.

Artist's Statement

In my visual art, I'm trying to express a tension between reality and fiction or between realism and artificiality, creating a style that is completely mine. Poser is the foundation for my digital art. My images have an entirely digital origin. None is based on a real model. Also, I don't use photos or photo manipulation. Combining the tools of Poser and Photoshop enables me to create any image I have in mind.

Influences

For my free art (not free-form art, but art that is not made under commission), I generally obtain my inspiration from real life: people around me, situations around me, or actual occurrences. This is art that is created without influence from sponsors or finance people.

Techniques

The Creative Process

Even as a child, I created art. Not creating art today would be like living without arms or legs. In most cases, I begin working without having a clear idea about what to create or how to create it. I start with an atmosphere or an emotion. I like working with Poser because it enables me to get human shapes or animals into the right proportions, no matter what kind of position I have them in. It's always an adventure to express these feelings in an image, which arises gradually after I've started the creative process.

Step-by-Step Tutorial: "Autumn Dance"

With the image "Autumn Dance" in Figure 2.8, I honor my best friend, Freek Kleijn, who died this year at the age of 46. The image characterizes him well: an artist and dancer in full bloom, passing away to another world.

1. In Figure 2.1, I start with DAZ's Victoria 3 (V3) figure in Poser. I play with the parameters until I find the facial expression I am looking for and the appropriate proportions for the body. I then scale the headdress prop to fit her head.

2. I fix the headdress prop on the subject's head by choosing the Object menu, Change Parent, and selecting Head from the figure hierarchy to ensure that the prop will automatically follow the pose of V3. See Figure 2.2.

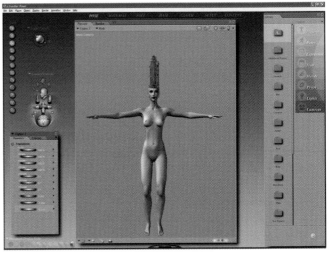

Figure 2.1 Find the right proportions and expression.

Figure 2.2 Make the head the parent of the headdress prop.

3. I set the light on standard position because I know I will do further work in Photoshop. In the Material room, I blacken the legs, hands, and so on by setting Diffuse Color to black and adding Glossy to Refraction Color. Then I render the result and save it as a PSD file. See Figure 2.3.

> **TIP**
>
> The Material room is one of the many tabbed rooms in Poser's interface. It's where color, texture, and other surface properties are assigned to the 3D objects.

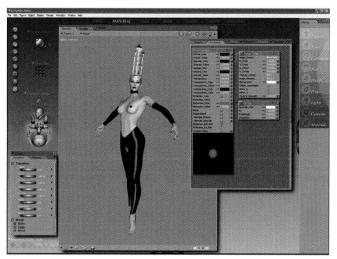

Figure 2.3 Using the Material room.

4. I create the shadows, background, and clothing in Photoshop. I copy V3 so that I can cut the headdress prop from the head, put it in the background, and make earrings from it. I merge the result into one layer and then copy it. See Figure 2.4.

Figure 2.4 Build the picture in Photoshop.

5. Using NixColor Efex Pro 2.0, I apply different filters to the layer, including Class Soft Focus and Brilliance. Then I use the filter BW Tonal Enhancer to set the layer to Dark. See Figure 2.5.

CARINA DUMAIS

ILLUSTRATION/SCI-FI FANTASY

Figure 2.5 Use Photoshop filters to enhance the image.

Figure 2.6 Deepen the color.

6. I apply the filter Bio Color Green Brown from NicColor to color the image a little deeper. Then I set the blending mode of the layer on Vivid Light, with Fill set to 58. See Figure 2.6.

7. To create depth, I use the Depth of Field filter that comes from the Digital Film Tools 55mm v6 Photoshop Filters plug-in set. I set the Fill value to 54. With this filter, the amount of blurring is proportional to the light values of the selection. To get the appropriate depth, I erase parts of the dark surface to different gradations using a soft brush set to a Hardness setting of 25. See Figure 2.7.

8. To finish, I add a bird and leaves that I rendered in Poser. I give the leaves a gradient treatment in Photoshop. See Figure 2.8.

Figure 2.7 Depth of Field filter.

Figure 2.8 "Autumn Dance" final image.

Insights

Lighting

Generally, I use the standard Poser lighting. Other times, I add some extra light to a scene or change the light's color or direction. After that, I render the scene many times—each time with different light colors and directions—and store them as Photoshop files. This enables me to use these different lighting scenes separately within Photoshop, which yields special results. It also allows the final lighting of the scene to be created by manipulating layers in Photoshop, possibly creating effects that might not be achievable by rendering in Poser alone.

Content

The Poser stock content makes it easy to create interesting images. Sometimes I buy several types of poses and props, but I can't resist changing them, especially their textures. Some of my favorite images are Victoria 3, children, and animals. When I need content for a project, I try to find it, no matter who the creator is. There are many content providers that have figures, models, props, and so on for purchase and for free that allow for an almost infinite amount of content to use for projects and images.

Posing Figures

Posing the figure comes first. Creating gestures and expressions is easy. When I start an image, I do not know what the final image will be like. I develop the figure's poses, gestures, and expressions while working intuitively.

Rendering

I usually render at 2657×3636 pixels and at 300 dpi. This is a good format for printing big posters. I enable Raytracing and Remove Backfacing Polygons.

TIP

Keep it simple! Start with small renders, simple images, and lots of practice to discover the possibilities of Poser. But beware of becoming addicted to Poser like I am.

Q&A

Where do you think computer-generated imagery will be 5–10 years from now?

Digital art in the future will be more important for the art scene than all traditional tools have been in the past. Creating computer-generated imagery will be an essential part of the curriculum of all art academies. I'm waiting desperately for a Poser version in Dutch!

What is the biggest challenge you have faced while using Poser?

The biggest challenge I have faced while using Poser has been an open-air project for the town center of Vlissingen, a rather small but international world harbor in the Netherlands. This project highlighted 25 big art pieces of mine, each 1.35×1.35 meters, that were exposed in the streets. The Poser pieces formed a route that guided the people to shops, companies, or organizations that were in the town center. Visitors could win prizes if they could name which Poser image was associated with each shop. I designed the 25 images with Poser at 5315×5315 pixels at 1500 dpi to produce big, high-quality prints. Figure 2.9 shows photos of several of the images that were installed throughout the Vlissingen Town Centre area.

CARINA DUMAIS

Figure 2.9 Vlissingen Town Centre outdoor Poser installation pieces.

ILLUSTRATION/SCI-FI FANTASY

NOTE

You can find complete documentation of this project on the German Web site http://www.expokult.net/europa/vlissingen/2005_art_route/2005_art_route_quellen.htm.

Resources

On the DVD

- Artist Gallery
- Photos: Vlissingen Town Centre outdoor Poser gallery installation
- Video: Fashion Art Performance, Vlissingen, The Netherlands

Links

- http://www.renderosity.com
- http://www.runtimedna.com
- http://www.contentparadise.com
- http://www.zs3d.com

CARINA DUMAIS

Studio

Software: Photoshop, Poser
Hardware: Windows XP

Contact

Carina Dumais ■ Vlissingen, The Netherlands ■ cdumais@zeelandnet.nl ■ http://people.zeelandnet.nl/cdumais

Gallery

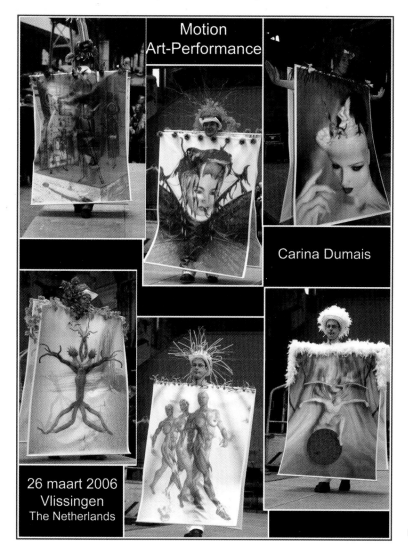

Motion Art-Performance

Carina Dumais

26 maart 2006
Vlissingen
The Netherlands

Fashion Art Performance, Vlissingen, The Netherlands.

ILLUSTRATION/SCI-FI FANTASY

"Factory."

"50+ Thinking of the Past."

CARINA DUMAIS

ILLUSTRATION/SCI-FI FANTASY

"Katja."

"I Don't Agree."

CARINA DUMAIS

"Look Inside."

"No Name."

"Garden in Love."

"The Beauty of Age."

KEVIN AIRGID

About the Artist

Kevin Airgid is an internationally recognized designer, author, and speaker. He runs a small interactive studio that develops creative projects for clients such as Amnesty International, ESPN, CBC News, and Lexus. He is the recipient of several national design awards and has been featured in the Macromedia Showcase, G4 Tech TV, *Digital Creative Arts* magazine, and *Communication Arts*. He is the author of several Web design books, the most recent being *Web Designer's Success Guide: How to Profit from Freelance Web Design*. He has written and lectured about Web design for various organizations around the world. He holds a degree in visual arts from the University of Western Ontario.

Artist's Statement

It is easy to get out of bed in the morning knowing that I am doing something positive. I use coffee and techno music to get the creative juices flowing. I also am always checking out Web sites and creative magazines for inspiration.

Influences

My motivation comes from working with social and human rights groups. I was influenced by the early days of interactive CD-ROM and Interactive TV. It was a new and exciting period for me that opened me up to so many possibilities and opportunities. I was also an early user of Flash software. I started using it when the first version was released. Regarding influential artists, Salvador Dali is on the top of my list. He was so psychedelic.

Techniques

The Creative Process

Over the years, I have learned that keeping my clients coming back for more involves producing quality work in a timely manner. Timelines for all my projects are short. It becomes more and more difficult to produce quality work in shorter and shorter periods, which is why using Poser has been such a successful endeavor for me. Poser enables me to produce sprites (animated objects and characters in games) in extremely short periods. The thing I love about Poser is the fact that I can drop some prebuilt animation sequences (such as a walk or run cycle) onto a character, render it, and export it out for Flash.

> **TIP**
>
> To render a scene to be imported to Flash, choose to save the image as a PNG file so that when the image is opened in Photoshop, it is automatically masked out.

Step-by-Step Tutorial: How I Use Poser for 3D Sprites in Games

A good example of how I use Poser for my Flash game creation is on a project I did for ESPN. This online 3D game was created for ESPN to help promote the Dr Pepper Championship Pass. This promotion featured an offline competition in which fans would have the opportunity to throw a football into a Dr Pepper can during halftime to win money. ESPN wanted to continue the promotion online using an advert-game to accomplish the same thing.

1. I start the project by slightly altering a stock Poser character. During the build-out of the character, I start with a character wearing shorts and a T-shirt, as shown in Figure 3.1. But the client wants me to change the character into blue jeans so he'll look more like a regular football fan.

Figure 3.1 This stock Poser character is easy to change as per client requests.

2. The apparel change doesn't take long. I just switch the clothes, as you can see in Figure 3.2. This is the beauty of Poser for online game development. Changing objects in a scene like this takes seconds instead of hours like it would in other applications.

Figure 3.2 After wardrobe change.

TIP

Another trick to making stock 3D items more unique is to edit the texture map of the object. Companies love to have their logos plastered on objects anywhere they can. It helps build the brand.

3. I edit the texture map of the football and apply the Dr Pepper logo to give it the custom feel. See Figure 3.3.

Figure 3.3 Custom footballs always help build the brand.

4. I render assets like the football and figure larger than necessary for the game. I use them to build the micro-site, shown in Figure 3.4. This saves time by eliminating the search for stock images or other media for the project.

Figure 3.4 Reuse of the 3D renders helps tie the project together.

5. During the development of the game, I merge the 3D characters with a real-world photo of a football stadium. I use stock 3D objects such as a biplane, hawk, and other objects to help distract the player from hitting the Dr Pepper can. See Figure 3.5.

Figure 3.5 The game interface with sprites created in Poser.

6. Overall, this game is a great success. The characters are easy to produce; I simply render them in Poser and then export them to alpha-transparent PNG sequences. After that, I import the sequences into Flash, and my programmer applies game logic to the animation. The total project takes just under 5 weeks to complete. You can view a live working version of the game at http://www.airgid.com/.

Insights

Lighting

I need flat, even lighting with no shadows. This way, I can import it into my Flash scene or project without problems.

Content

Stock figures are important to me. I don't have time to make my own figures, and it is so easy and cost effective to get the figures online from Content Paradise or DAZ. I use the stock figures for simple animations such as when the characters are throwing or running.

Q&A

What advice do you have for artists who are starting out with Poser?

New Poser users should start with the basics and not put too many objects in the scene. Light and render the scene with one or just a few objects, and gradually work your way up.

Where do you think computer-generated imagery will be 5–10 years from now?

I think that 10 years from now, it will be nothing like it is now. It will involve the human senses. I imagine it will be more like the movie *The Matrix*.

Resources

Links

- http://pixelsurgeon.com/
- http://www.amnesty.org
- http://www.thefwa.com
- http://www.crossminds.com

KEVIN AIRGID

Studio

Software: Poser, Photoshop, Flash, Dreamweaver, Illustrator, Particle Illusion

Hardware: Dual-monitor Pentium system with 2 gigs of RAM

Contact

Kevin Airgid ▪ Airgid Media Inc. ▪ Tecumseh, Ontario ▪ http://www.airgid.com

BRIAN JON HABERLIN

About the Artist

Brian has been making and breaking his own rules as a professional comic illustrator since he began at age 18 and taught himself computer graphics. He became known as a creator of the popular *Witchblade* comic book. Brian is an innovator of many modern production and computer art methods used in the comic industry and is regarded by many as a digital guru. He was featured on an episode of the *How'd They Do That?* television show demonstrating his process. Avalon Studios, which he created in 1998, has worked on anywhere from 1–4 titles in the top 10 of the comic industry every month, and Brian and his studio have been nominated for and received many comic industry awards. Some of those awards include the Eisner Award, Best CD cover (for *Korn Follow the Leader*), Society of Illustrators West, and many others. Brian's work was recently added to the permanent collection at The Smithsonian in Washington, D.C.

Artist's Statement

I get bored easily and have a short attention span. Armed with that, I am constantly creating new images and techniques. Once I figure out, "Oh, I can do that now," I move on to other styles and subjects. But people who know me seem to be able to recognize my work even when I've switched a style. I guess styles and techniques are just the surface. The substance that is always the same in my work is emotion. Whether brooding or playful, emotion is what art is all about.

Influences

I'm a sponge creatively. I love looking at everyone's work and taking away something from it—not that I like it all, but there will be bits and pieces. I might really like the way one artist did his clouds or really like the pattern detail she accomplished in her piece. The list of artists who have influenced me is far too long to mention here. I have a library of over a thousand art books, and I'd have to mention them all.

"Meditation."

COMIC/CARTOON

Techniques

The Creative Process

Before jumping on the computer, you *must* have a road map. I start with good old pencil and paper and highly recommend keeping a sketchbook. I know, I know. You've heard it a million times before, but a sketchbook helps keep your ideas from floating away and provides a good library as to your personal artistic journey. I do a lot of sketching and then jump on and off the computer for most of my pieces, sometimes working over printouts with gouache or oils and then scanning back in. The more I can get my hands dirty, the more I like it.

Another reason for the road map is that it's easy to burn hours just playing with a pose or lighting or texturing. There are so many choices to be made with 3D. Poser is like having your own modeling agency, costume shop, special effects studio, and prop shop in your own home.

Step-by-Step Tutorial: Creating the Image "Hair"

1. Figure 4.1 shows my first sketches for this design. I kind of know what I want before I start sketching/doodling, but a sketch helps me nail down the design. I only do a couple of quick sketches. I want the design to focus on the hair.

2. After I decide on the basic design, I further refine the sketch. You'll notice details in Figure 4.2 that did not make it to the final. For example, the subject has less clothing here and details that are in the final that are not here. That's okay. The sketches serve as a road map only. The sketches shouldn't be so tight and detailed that they bind the creativity.

Figure 4.1 Sketch out the design on paper as a roadmap.

Figure 4.2 Let go with the sketch; don't let it bind your creativity.

> **TIP**
>
> When doing portraits in Poser, change the camera's focal length to 75mm or higher to minimize distortions from the figure.

3. Once I have an idea for the basic design, I fire up Poser. I pose the figure, set up the lights, dress her, and render. I try to be as down and dirty as possible about using 3D applications, because I feel the work only comes to life after being stepped on by hand or by a hand with a stylus in a paint program.

In the close-up raw render in Figure 4.3, the skin texture is not quite right. The fingers look a bit broken, and the hair is definitely not what will be the final. But it's a good starting point.

My motto is to fix it in post! It's faster and more fun that way.

> **TIP**
>
> Render as high a resolution as your machine allows so that you have more options in post.

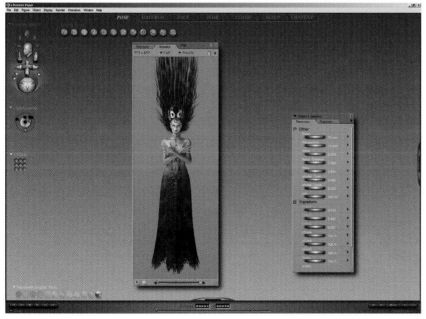

Figure 4.3 Rough out your Poser figure; the details will be fixed in post.

COMIC/CARTOON

4. In Figure 4.4, I move the render into Photoshop. The first thing I want to do is pump up the volume on the figure's hair. She needs more—much more! I select her hair and go into the Liquify filter. I use a big brush and just start pushing and pulling the hair closer to my original design.

NOTE

If you are not familiar with the Liquify tool, it basically turns your image into a live putty-like surface that you can move around and distort without smearing. Liquify is one of my favorite tools for fixing eye placement or reshaping a figure.

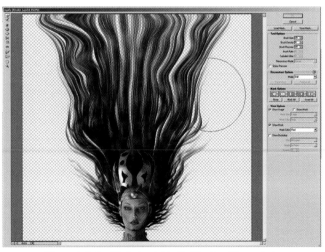

Figure 4.4 Use Photoshop's Liquify filter to add more hair.

5. Okay, I got wider hair, but I need more. The easiest solution is to copy and paste what I already have into another layer. See Figure 4.5. I copy the head and hair twice to two different layers. Then, on each layer, I use the Free Transform tool and resize and rotate so that on one layer will be the right side extra hair and the other the left. Next, I place them behind the render. The model now has lots more hair. If anything is showing through that I don't want from those underlying layers, I just erase it.

6. Okay, this is my thing, probably from my love of comic book art or even old poster art like Alphonse Mucha. I start creating a holding line around my figure. If you want to do this automatically, you can simply load the alpha channel that Poser creates and stroke it in Photoshop. Sometimes that gets you where you want to go. But here I have a lot of hair, and that doesn't stroke too well. The hair uses a lot of transparency to create a sense of softness at the edges; making a hard-edged line around the hair might ruin the effect. So I use the stroke in some places and hand-draw it in others using the Brush tool with a hard-edged brush. See my version in Figure 4.6.

7. In Figure 4.7, I use a glamour photography trick to soften the model but not lose too much detail. The trick involves copying the layer with the image on it (flatten it if you have to) and then pasting it in another layer. Use the Gaussian Blur filter at about 10 pixels and lower the opacity of the layer to about 30 percent. The result of the render is an old movie star gloss and odd pixels that are smoothed out.

I copy that blurred layer again, place it uppermost in the layers, and change its mode to Overlay at about 50 percent, which helps bring back some of the color richness. I also add a black background.

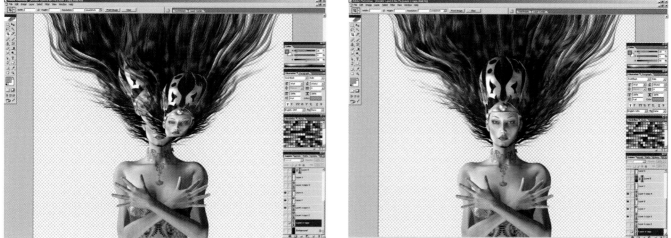

Figure 4.5 Copy the head twice to create more hair; erase the parts that don't belong.

Figure 4.6 Create a holding line around the figure.

Figure 4.7 Use a glamour photography trick to soften the figure without losing detail.

8. I want to add a design element. Mucha uses all kind of star imagery, and if it's good enough for him… Figure 4.8 uses the star shape from the custom shapes under the Pen tool. I make one and then copy, paste, and rotate each into position in a circle. I apply a scanned texture that I made to grunge up the star a bit.

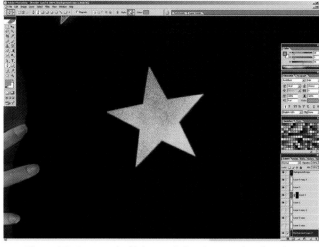

Figure 4.8 Create and add the star design element using Photoshop.

9. Now it's time for details, starting with her face. The model looks a little too stern. I use the Liquify filter to make her expression a bit more playful. See Figure 4.9 for the before and after.

10. The last bit to do is to add interesting fingernails. I go back into Poser and give the model some nails with a morph. I rerender and paste the new fingertips over the old ones, adjusting as needed with Levels to match. See Figure 4.10.

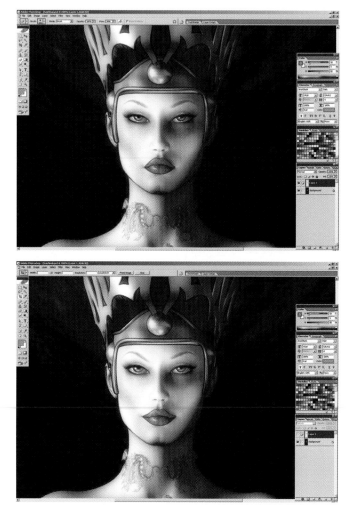

Figure 4.9 Before and after: Use the Liquify filter in Photoshop to alter the expression.

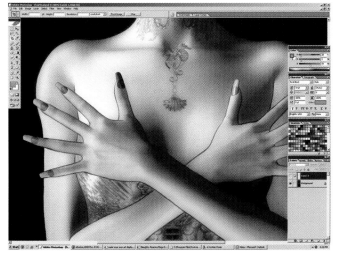

Figure 4.10 Add the blue fingernails for the finishing touch.

TIP

Remember to save the PZ3 file of your final render. That makes it easy to change elements—such as longer fingernails I added at the end of this piece—and composite onto the original render in post.

11. She's done. Figure 4.11 is the final image.

Figure 4.11 "Hair" final image.

BRIAN JON HABERLIN

Step-by-Step Tutorial: "Meditation"

1. For "Meditation" (see Figure 4.19), as usual, I start with pen and paper. I'm after an image that reflects our heroine's powers of concentration and speed. She is to be the "eye of the storm." I really have the image quite clearly in my head, so I do only the one sketch in Figure 4.12.

   This is going to be a complex scene, so rather than overload Poser with a ton of geometry all at once, I load in the various elements separately to composite in Photoshop later. To do this, it's necessary to know a bit about perspective. I keep it simple by establishing a horizon line and then "hang" everything around that.

Figure 4.12 Sketch the design and establish a horizon for perspective.

> ### TIP
>
> **Render elements separately for speed. The more models you load into Poser, the longer it takes, and the more system resources it demands. If you have a design to follow and keep your camera in the same place, it becomes easy to position images in the scene where they should be and then composite them later.**

2. In Figure 4.13, I start rendering background to foreground. That way, I can also use the background render as reference for figure placement. In my mind, I'm pretty sure I'm going to do a lot of blurring to this piece, so I'm not too concerned with the detail of my background models. In the unblurred render, I'm even using Poser 4 figures for far background figures. Hey, they're memory light and fast to work with, and because I plan to blur them later, I know from previous experience that using a super-high-res model in their place is a waste. It's important to keep the lighting the same so that the direction of the light doesn't shift from element to element. The same goes for focal length.

> ### TIP
>
> **When checking your composition, render tests at low resolution. This way everything goes faster, and you can double-check your composition. When you're satisfied, crank up the resolution.**

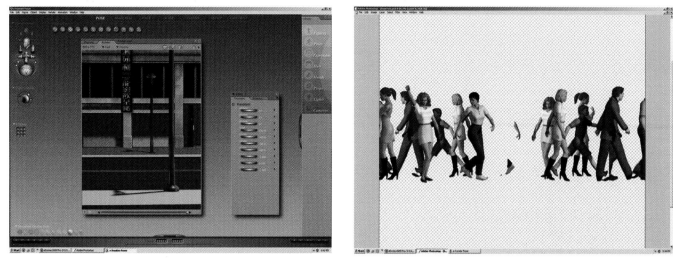

Figure 4.13 Render separate layers of figures, working from background to foreground.

3. I render six layers of figures for this image. In Figure 4.14, they are shown as straight unretouched renders without the background.

4. Here comes the fun part—putting all the pieces together and tweaking. To give our heroine that "I'm about to kick your ass" serenity, I motion blur all around her. See Figure 4.15. The rule here is that the closer the object is to our main character, the less it is motion blurred; the farther away, the more it is blurred. This effect also helps to give great depth to the piece. I also add a few birds to the piece and add shadows in a Multiply layer to ground some of the characters.

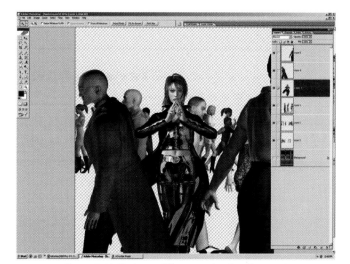

Figure 4.14 Six layers of figures rendered and imported into Photoshop for compositing.

BRIAN JON HABERLIN

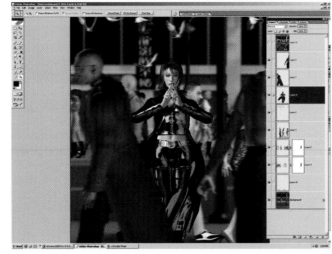

Figure 4.15 Blurring the image to create depth and motion.

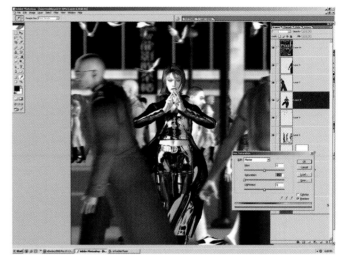

Figure 4.16 Use Hue/Saturation, Desaturate to make the piece grayscale.

> ## TIP
>
> **Put detail where it matters most. If everything in your pictures has the same level of detail, nothing stands out. Use detail as you would light, shadow, or color to help focus the attention of your viewer to what matters most.**

5. By the way, did I mention that this piece is going to eventually be grayscale? It will be like one of those cool black-and-white photos from the '50s, like that one of James Dean walking down a wet city street. I copy a flattened version of the piece into the upper-most layer and use Desaturate (found within Image, Adjustments) to strip the color from the piece. See Figure 4.16.

6. Figure 4.17 shows how the piece comes together. I use a thin/hard Airbrush tool to outline my main figure and to heighten detail. I also add (in the image on the right) a pencil on paper texture that I did covering an 11×17 piece of paper and scanned in. I apply that over the grayscale image in Overlay mode. It gives the image a hand-drawn sort of grain and makes my airbrush touchups look like natural pencil.

> ## TIP
>
> **To even out retouching, add some texture or grain over the entire piece. That fools the eye into making the image surface look consistent.**

COMIC/CARTOON

Figure 4.17 Scan in a paper texture and apply it in Overlay mode to create a hand-drawn effect.

Figure 4.18 Notice the varnished blacks.

7. Now I just want to punch up the image a little more and smooth it out a bit. I do this first by flattening the image. Then I copy that image to a new layer. I Guassian blur this layer about 10 pixels and set it to 18 percent opacity. That helps to soften the model a bit, but for the punch, I copy that layer again and put it uppermost in the layer sandwich in Overlay mode at 40 percent. It gives my blacks more punch—almost like adding a varnish on a painting. Look at these details in Figure 4.18. And she's done! See Figure 4.19 for the final image.

Figure 4.19 "Meditation": the final image.

COMIC/CARTOON

Insights

Lighting

On a basic level, lighting should help the viewer to see the subject and complement it aesthetically. I keep it pretty simple using only one or two lights. Typically, I just use a main light and a kicker. One is shadow casting, the other not. This gives me a lot of speed when rendering.

Content

If you know what you're doing, you can mix and match a lot of unique figures from the stock Poser content. Give me James and the Face room alone, and I can cast quite a comic. When I need other content, I usually can find it at Content Paradise, Renderosity, DAZ 3D, Runtime DNA, or Poser World. Some of my favorite content creators are Billy-T, Sanctum Art, Blackhearted, As Shanim, Danie and marforno, Morris, Stonemason, Sixus1, Xurge 3D, BatLab, and dozens more. It is a super-talented community of creators.

Q&A

What are the hardest postures, gestures, and expressions to create? Why?
The hardest thing is to make your poses and expressions natural. The best solution is a mirror. If you don't or can't pose that way, it's a tip that something is wrong with your model's pose.

What advice do you have for artists who are starting out with Poser?
Save—often. Work from small to big. In other words, first render small to check things before wasting time on a full-resolution render. And fix things in post. If you try to get the perfect render, it eats your time. You can waste hours just experimenting with lighting. By having to fix things, you're forced to add more of your own style and touch to a piece.

What do you think will be most significant in CGI 5–10 years from now?
I think it will just get more and more intuitive and easy to use. Probably some new form will be available, like very real holograms. I look forward to the day that I can just imagine the art in my head and it will appear onscreen or as a sculpture.

Resources

On the DVD

- Artist Gallery
- Three digital art tutorial videos: "Adding Eye Glow," "Adding Stars and Snow," and "Adding Effects"
- Six Photoshop PSD files and dozens of free effects that accompany the tutorials

Links

- http://www.goodbrush.com

BRIAN JON HABERLIN

Studio

Software: Poser, Photoshop, Painter, Vue

Hardware: Custom-built machine with 3GB of RAM and a Wacom Cintiq 21x

Contact

Brian Jon Haberlin ■ Avalon Studios/Haberlin Studios ■ Laguna Niguel, CA ■ haberlinstudios@aol.com ■ http://www.digitalarttutorials.com ■ http://www.haberlin.com

Gallery

"Barbarians Cover."

"Hair."

BRIAN JON HABERLIN

"Candy."

"Cel."

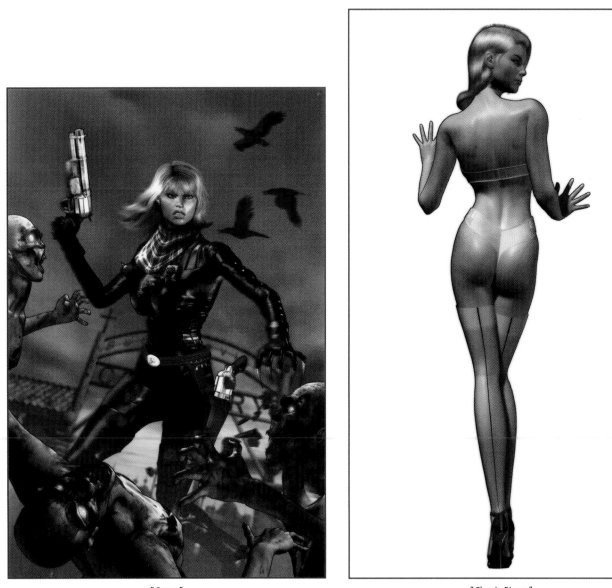

"Cover."

"Classic Pinup."

"Clip."

"Cross2."

"Dragons."

COMIC/CARTOON

"Hair 2."

"Haven."

"Heroes."

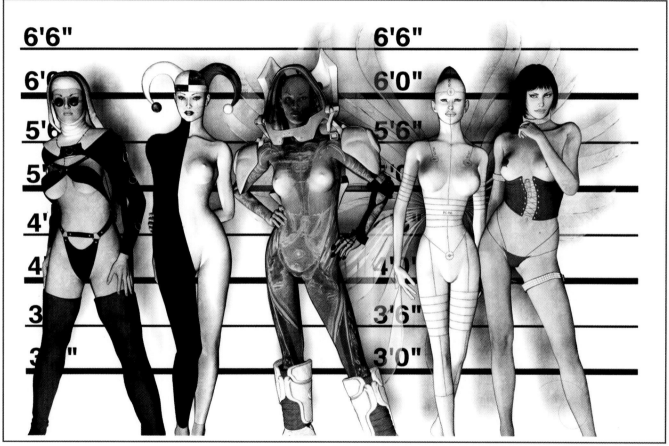

"Lineup."

COMIC/CARTOON

"Page 1 Chick Fight."

"Page 2 Chick Fight."

"Quick Paint Part 3."

"Shi Final."

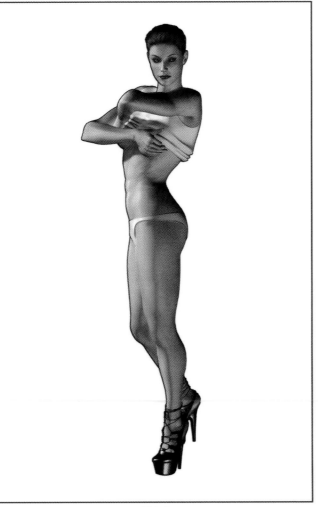

"Shirt."

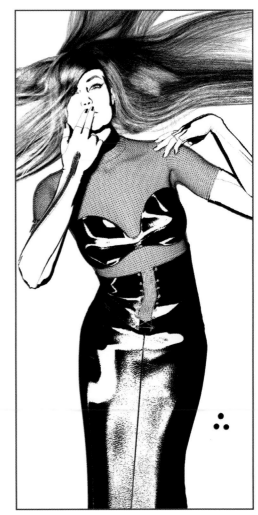

"Smiler."

BRIAN JON HABERLIN

"Unexpected Knight."

"Untitled-2."

"Untitled-3."

"Untitled-7."

"Whitehair."

"Whitequeen."

DANIEL SCOTT GABRIEL MURRAY

About the Artist

Daniel Scott Gabriel Murray is a cartoonist because he wants to be. He enjoys his time and strives to go bigger and better. His images will move you. He went to school for a while at The University of the Arts, in Philadelphia, and he has read lots of books. He also enjoys going to conventions. His career highlights so far include working with DC Comics, being the lead artist for Grand Virtual Gaming, and doing lots of freelance work.

Artist's Statement

I render what I like. I like dynamics, movement, emotion, characters. I try to capture that feeling of when I was seven watching *Jonny Quest* for the first time. I am fortunate that I can retain that feeling of wonder even though I'm grown.

Influences

Doug Wildey, creator of *Jonny Quest*, was most likely the single most influential person in my young life. Re-creating his adventures is what started me drawing. Later I was influenced by Frank Frazetta, an American original master of fantasy illustration. Frank is unmatched in his ability to capture passion, grace, and fire in a brushstroke. I haven't found a greater instructor on how to make an illustration, painting, or rendering come alive. There are technically more adept painters, but no one will ever match his elegance.

Others influences include Jim Steranko, Rick Bryant, Howie Chakin, Alex Ross, Dave Devries, John Romita, Bernie Wrightson, Jeffrey Jones, Maxfield Parrish, Tex Avery, Chuck Jones—basically everyone who's ever walked the planet. Motivations? I create images that make me happy. It's that simple.

"Duo."

Techniques

The Creative Process

Poser is the start, and generally, it's the core application that I use for my work. From there, it's about knowing how to extract that vision from your head and translate it into terms that software can understand. I get a visual in my head, and then I push-pull-click-clack inside the programs to get the ball rolling. Usually I hate it and start again; then I hate that, too. Finally, I come up with something I hate less and start building from there. Finally, Photoshop fixes a pile of evil to produce something that's most likely 40 percent at best of what I saw initially.

Step-by-Step Tutorial: Creating "Vertigo"

Certain things, such as lighting, texturing, transparency, and high dynamic range imaging (HDRI), can be taught. HDRI allows for a greater dynamic range of exposures (a large difference between dark and light areas) that represents the wide range of intensity and can really make your images lifelike.

But other things can never be taught. For instance, how can I tell you how to pose a figure or what camera setting to use? How do I explain what makes an image dynamic or eye catching or show you drama? How can I teach you how to take the vision in your head and translate it through the software you're using? In the following tutorial, I'll do my best to show you how I accomplish these goals. Hopefully you can glean something from my methods.

1. I start with a vision from my rattletrap that I call a mind. I have an excellent idea of what I want to see and a half-baked idea of how to make it visual. From there, I figure out what elements I need and where I need to make them. For "Vertigo" (see Figure 5.1), I used Poser for the Ghost figure and 3ds Max for the city shot. Why use Max? I already had a simple city built in it. Could I do it in Poser? Sure, but why reinvent the wheel? I use lots of software for different tasks. Specialization is for insects.

Figure 5.1 Use your tools, improvise, and adapt.

2. In Figure 5.2, I have the beginnings of each element of the scene. For clarity's sake, I exclude the background on the Poser figure. In Figure 5.3, I render a smaller version of the cityscape to get my perspective correct for the figure. The camera's focal length is set to 30mm.

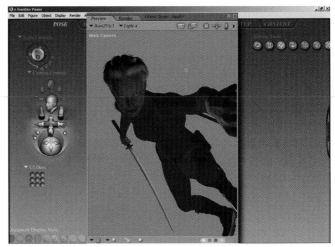

Figure 5.2 Exclude the background from the Poser figure.

COMIC/CARTOON

TIP

Experiment. If you want to stand out from everyone else, don't look like everyone else. Many folks never change the out-of-the-box settings that come with Poser. Go nuts! Foreshorten, extend, extrude, bend, fold, spindle, and mutilate.

NOTE

If I use multiple figures in an image, I render them separately for greater control of the lighting.

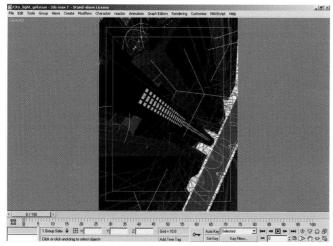

Figure 5.3 Render the background smaller to establish perspective.

Figure 5.4 Light the Poser figure.

3. Figure 5.4 is the raw figure. As with most of my images, I use four lights on the Ghost figure: one front ambient occlusion, two on each side, and one rear above. I drop the front light to about 70 percent to let the rear lights achieve their effect.

4. I render the cityscape in 3ds Max. I'm not worried about making things perfect at this point. The art has a hint of what I want. I drop the cityscape background into a Photoshop document and work on the figure next. Figure 5.5 is the raw render out of Max.

5. In Figure 5.6, I render the Poser figure as a TIF file. One of Poser's output advantages is that it renders the alpha channel with its TIF output. For folks like me who composite their images, the alpha channel is an essential and timesaving tool. Next, I separate the figure and image and drop the figure into a Photoshop document.

COMIC/CARTOON

Figure 5.5 Render the background in 3ds Max.

Figure 5.6 Render the Poser figure as a TIF file.

Figure 5.7 Copy the original layers.

6. In Figure 5.7, I am working in Photoshop, where I now have two layers: the cityscape background and the Poser figure. I copy both of them. I always make copies of my original layers.

7. In Figure 5.8, I use the Transform tool on the working background layer and select Warp. Distorting the background simulates a lens distortion, which gives a better feeling of height to the image.

Hair

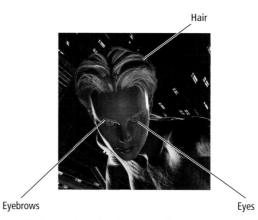

Eyebrows   Eyes

Figure 5.9 Post work needs to be done on the eyes, eyebrows, and hair.

9. In Figure 5.10, I use the Dodge tool and brighten those dull eyes.

TIP

The eyes are the window to the soul. If your eyes look alive, the rest of your render will follow. Search for a photo reference, or look in a mirror. Life is through the eyes.

Figure 5.8 Distorting the image creates a feeling of height.

8. I begin working on the figure. I'm concentrating on the head to start, and then I will apply the same techniques to other parts of her frame. In the next few steps, I will work on her eyes, eyebrows, and hair. Figure 5.9 shows how dark these three features are before being worked on.

10. In Figure 5.11, I set the Smudge tool to a small brush size to change blobs of partly rendered eyebrows into something useful. Actually, I could use a trans map on the eyebrow model and avoid this step.

DANIEL SCOTT GABRIEL MURRAY

Dodge tool for eye highlights and form

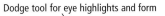

Figure 5.10 Bring life to the eyes with the Dodge tool.

Smudge tool for small hairs

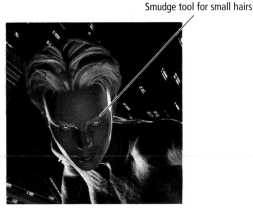

Figure 5.11 Fix the poorly rendered eyebrows using the Smudge tool (or a trans map).

11. In Figure 5.12, I use the Dodge tool again to brighten the light coming through Ghost's hair from the city below. For the forefront of her hair, I use the Burn tool to darken and shade the area. Even though the image isn't finished, I'm starting to see the difference. I'll blur and adjust the edges of her hair with the Smudge tool in the final pass.

Burn tool for dark areas   Dodge tool for backlighting

Figure 5.12 Deepen the hair with the Dodge and Burn tools.

12. In Figure 5.13, I apply the techniques from the past few steps across Ghost's frame to enhance the dynamics overall.

13. Using the now famous Dodge tool, I widen the brush and attack the city. Having defeated its citizens and claimed dominion and lordship over them… oh, sorry. Flashback.

In Figure 5.14, I use the Dodge tool to bring out the lights from the ground below. I get the glow to a level I can stand, and then I add a bit of airbrush to the windows for effect and generally blur the ground, street, and headlights for atmosphere rather than detail. Ghost is the focus. Everything else is filler to support her.

Figure 5.13 Reapply the technique across the frame of the figure.

Figure 5.14 Dodge and blur the background to support the figure as the focus of the image.

14. The elements are now in place. In Figure 5.15, I add a new layer on top of everything else and add glow to Ghost's hair and whatever else I think needs a boost. Finally, I stroke the figure in a 3-pixel black outline à la Adam Hughes.

Figure 5.15 Add a new layer and then apply glow and an outline.

15. Figure 5.16 is the final pass, and it is close to the vision I see in my head. The final "Vertigo" image is Figure 5.17.

DANIEL SCOTT GABRIEL MURRAY

75

Figure 5.16 How do you know when an image is complete?

Figure 5.17 "Vertigo" final image.

Insights

Lighting

I got a copy of a particular shader script made for Poser. From there, I tweaked, screamed, and sacrificed several farm animals to get a shader node that does what I want. I generally work with four lights: one front (usually ambient occlusion) and three point lights behind. I render each figure separately so that I can control each "thing" and deal with interaction later. I use dramatic rim lighting and just a hair of reduced front light for drama.

Content

Stock figures have been far better as Poser has progressed. Jessie and James are really the first stock figures that I've used for production work. Content? I've got boatloads of parts, pieces, and stuff. I mix and match, morph, and retool. Again, I use whatever works.

Q&A

What are some of your timesaving tips when using Poser on a project or artwork?
I save "core" figures and call them up ad infinitum. With the shading system I use, it would take half an hour just to get the character up to speed. Knowing Poser's limits is another thing. It's a great program, but there are things that I can do faster in Photoshop—nothing spectacular, really, but things like superhero suits. Generally, I render characters gray or the basic costume colors and do the rest in Photoshop. It saves a boatload of time rather than screwing with texture mapping.

What are some of your favorite Poser features?
Ease of use is a big one. Models are prerigged, which saves me a pile-o-time. I have literally Gigs of models—Poser and otherwise—to create whatever thing I need at the time. Because I work in layers, rendering each figure separately, the alpha TIF output makes compositing a breeze.

What advice do you have for artists who are starting out with Poser?

Experiment, Experiment, Experiment. Find your passion and do it. Don't limit yourself within the program. I use it as a core, a tool. That's what Larry designed it for. Poser can do great things, and its render engine is very nice. But remember that Weta Digital [the LoTR folks] use multitudes of software to make magic. You can, too. This software is addictive, and you'll need a 12-step program to break the habit.

Where do you think computer-generated imagery will be 5–10 years from now?

Given the current rate of development in CPU horsepower and technology, major motion pictures will be developed on a home computer. In 15 years, most likely less, there'll be CGI superstars whom you'll never know only exist in a box, and America's heartthrob with only exist as 00100111010011. I can see Humphrey Bogart starring in a new release within 10 years.

What do you wish someone had told you when you started using Poser?

Use caution in your business dealings. Seek a competent copyright attorney. Seek information and professional advice on how to protect your work. I have the pleasure and extreme good fortune to call some of the comic industry's greatest names friends. All of them have horror stories of losing original works, rights, and royalties rightly owed to them because of shifty people. Protect your backside. Apart from that, have fun.

Resources

On the DVD

- Artist Gallery

Links

- http://www.frazettaartgallery.com/
- http://homepage.mac.com/rickjbryant/
- http://www.themonsterengine.com/
- http://www.billsienkiewicz.com/
- http://www.justsayah.com/
- http://www.earthcurves.com/
- http://www.elektralusion.com/

DANIEL SCOTT GABRIEL MURRAY

Studio

Software: Poser, 3ds Max, Photoshop
Hardware: P4, 3.1GHz with 2GB RAM, 256 dual video, Wacom tablet

Contact

Daniel Scott Gabriel Murray ▪ ALPC.com ▪ Gardiner, Maine
kahuna@alpc.com ▪ http://www.alpc.com

COMIC/CARTOON

Gallery

"Batgirl."

"Batman."

"Ghost."

"Dive."

COMIC/CARTOON

"Goth."

"Ivy."

"Nightmare."

"Wounded."

"Catwoman."

"Ghost."

DANIEL SCOTT GABRIEL MURRAY

COMIC/CARTOON

"Ghost."

"75 Yards."

"1000 Yards."

"Ghost."

DANIEL SCOTT GABRIEL MURRAY

LES GARNER

About the Artist

Les Garner is a highly respected self-taught artist who works as a graphics producer. Growing up, he read comic books voraciously and worked hard to emulate artists such as Neal Adams, Estaban Moroto, Jim Aparo, Gil Kane, Joe Kubert, Frank Frazetta, Tex Avery, and Ralph Bakshi. Upon graduation from high school and a short stint in college, Les spent a little over five years working for a number of independent comic book companies, focusing mostly on horror and science fiction. Along the way, he began moonlighting for various print and advertising agencies. Through interaction with them and due to the growing presence of technology in the comic book industry, Les developed an interest in computer graphics. At the same time, he was building his skills in airbrushing. Then he combined those airbrushing skills with his newfound passion for digital art. From there, his interests moved into 3D animation, where his focus has remained ever since, culminating in the creation, with his wife Rebekah, of their business, Sixus1 Media.

Artist's Statement

In terms of Poser, the majority of what I do is production work, providing content for others to use. The art of Poser for me is in designing new figures that might have a look or function to them to spur some creativity in the people who eventually use them. In terms of art in general, I am a hardcore anatomist: I love to study the machinery of people and animals, because whether you're doing still images or animation, modeling or character rigging, understanding those mechanics is integral to the believability of any type of character-oriented work.

Coming from a background in comic books and having most of my efforts now focused on animating, I try to stay conscious of composition and storytelling, no matter what the medium. Even in creating Poser figures that I might never get time to use beyond the point of their final release to the public, I try to think through the creature, animal, or character in a way that hopefully makes it feel as though it breathes, as though the creature has been somewhere and done something. That's probably the real heart of everything I turn out, regardless of what medium it's for. I try to make everything I do have an attitude that really conveys a personal history to the character.

"Dragon Ogre Attack."

Influences

Coming from a background in comic books and traditional illustration, my influences are mostly guys like Frank Frazetta, Joe Kubert, Jack Kirby, Todd McFarlane, Joe Quesada, Will Eisner, and Frank Miller. I would have to credit Joe Quesada and David Mack with being great influences beyond just their art. Back when I was doing a lot of comic conventions, I ran into those guys a lot and was lucky enough to get some really great input from them on my work at some early stages, from around age 19–22 or so. They really helped open up my thinking to a lot more about art than what I had considered up to that point. From them, I picked up an insane love of the artist Alphonse Mucha, a Czechoslovakian artist who ruled the Art Nouveau scene at the turn of the last century.

Beyond just my usual list of comic and illustration influences, I'd say my artwork is always heavily influenced by film. Storytelling and composition are the two most important aspects of any visual art, so I'm always rewatching movies from directors I admire to see how they set up the blocking of their shots, how they arrange the shapes throughout the frame and scene, how the story flows from one shot to another and even within a single frozen frame. When I'm doing still images, that's the goal: to make the image feel like I've just snagged it from the middle of a much larger, more involved sequence. I look to people like the Wachowski brothers, George Lucas, Tobe Hooper, Rob Zombie, Peter Jackson, and Robert Rodriguez. I'm also heavily into Asian cultures, especially Japanese, and I absolutely love the horror films from these regions. There's something very refreshing about films like the live-action *Devilman* from Go Nagai or a movie like *Samurai Resurrection*. The imagery in those is just incredible. Stepping back a generation or so, I really enjoy the works of Kurosawa; there's a real beauty in the photography and staging there.

Aside from all that, Rebekah and I both read quite a bit, which plays a big role in my work. H. P. Lovecraft has been a massive influence, as has Clive Barker for both his stories and art.

Word Made Flesh from Jack O'Connell is just about my favorite book ever, in part for its imagery and the way its descriptions managed to form images that have stuck in my brain in a bizarre way. I read a lot of philosophy, psychology, and sociology books, too. It's always good to know what the psychoanalysts will say about you when you're gone!

Techniques

The Creative Process

Draw. Draw a lot. Draw everything. Even if I plan to do something rendered in 3D, I draw at least a thumbnail design of it first. There is nothing that can replace the way a pencil and paper under my hands can drive my brain to explore and create. The computer and its software are just tools, and I don't deride them at all, but if all the electricity in the world suddenly vanished, I would still be happily trudging along with sticks and berries, scrawling beasties on a cave wall somewhere. Draw, draw, draw.

Far too many people allow the technology of 3D to become their crutch. I scratch something on paper, no matter how rough. And I swear, once I do that, it's almost like the paper talks back; it's like I need to stare into the fibers of that sheet, squeeze the pencil like a weapon, or stroke it like a lover and just see where my mind wanders. Traditional media give a rawness, a messiness, and a chaos that is the exact opposite of the computer. So while I love the tools of digital art, 3D, Poser, and Maya and all that can be accomplished with them, art starts with stick figures on a sheet of paper. If the thumbnail drawings feel alive, if their composition is solid, if the storytelling is obvious even in a really primitive state, then when you have finally translated that into a piece of rendered, digital art, the life you find in that beginning of primitive media will still be there. The final piece can end up being the best of both worlds: the look that only digital media can achieve, but with the raw heart and soul of traditional art.

Drawing is so integral to the way I think about art and animation; I pack sketchbooks full of stuff all the time. When I go out to eat, I find myself swiping my kids' crayons and doodling caricatures on the napkins of the other people in the place. Everything done on the computer is just an extension of drawing. Even people who think they draw poorly should still do it because of the way it opens up their thinking.

Step-by-Step Tutorial: The Dragon Ogre Attack

1. First I draw a quick sketch. Figure 6.1 is one of the rough sketches I work out to get an idea of just where I want to go with this piece. While a comparison of the sketch to the final image shows some definite deviations from the original concept, the sketch is still important in helping make decisions that guide all the work from there on out.

2. While only loosely indicated in the sketch, I know that I want the environment to be a kind of craggy, cave-like setting that might evoke a kind of dark, sword-and-sorcery feel. To build the cave, I use a series of extrusions to pull the basic shape from a flat polygonal plane in Maya. Then I use various cuts and subdivisions in the object's surface to build the rough form of the object. See Figure 6.2.

3. I texture the cave entirely inside Maya using procedural shaders that are baked out to a JPG file for use in Poser. The image in Figure 6.3 shows the texture node network I use to create the rough, stony surface of the cave.

Figure 6.1 Draw a rough sketch of the final image.

TIP

Baking is the term used for rendering procedural shaders to image files that can then be used as texture maps in any 3D application.

CONTENT

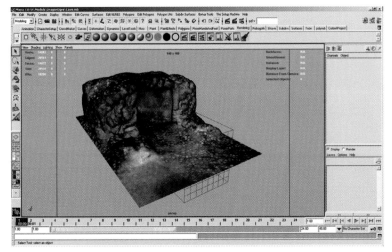

Figure 6.2 Build and shape the environment in Maya.

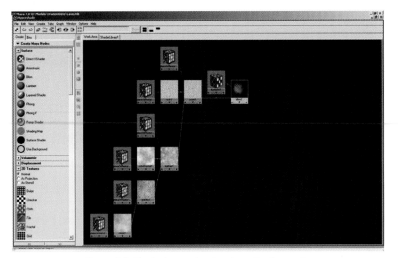

Figure 6.3 The texture node network creates the rough,
stony surface of the cave.

4. I sculpt further refinement of the mesh in ZBrush, as shown in Figure 6.4.

5. I save the cave as an OBJ file and import the file into Poser. I'm choosing the Dragon Ogre as the focus of this piece because it is a new figure that was a lot of fun to make. Figure 6.5 shows the Dragon Ogre loaded and positioned, with the Project Human Female on the defensive from different camera angles.

6. Figure 6.6 is a viewport capture that shows my positions of the figures and the composition for the final render. A major difference in the final image from the original sketch is the prominence of the female figure. While sketching, I envisioned something a little more traditional, with the female character seeming more victimized; however, after a few more drawings and some tinkering with the scene in Poser, she started to feel more like a warrior than a victim. In the end, I'm going with the idea that while the Dragon Ogre may be a deadly attacker, the heroine might just be able to handle that halberd well enough to hold her own!

7. I render the final elements in Poser and give them a bit of attention in Photoshop. I paint additional hair onto the female figure and use the Dodge and Burn tools in a number of places to add highlights and accenting. I paint in semitransparent layers of mist and fog and add an extension to the background that I sampled from renders of the topmost edge of the cave. Figure 6.7 is the final image.

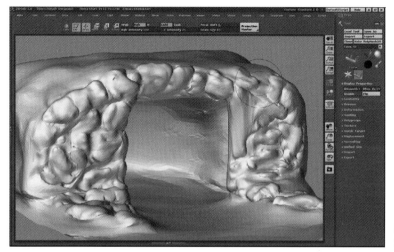

Figure 6.4
Sculpt the mesh in ZBrush.

Figure 6.5 The Dragon Ogre loaded and positioned, with the Project Human Female on the defensive.

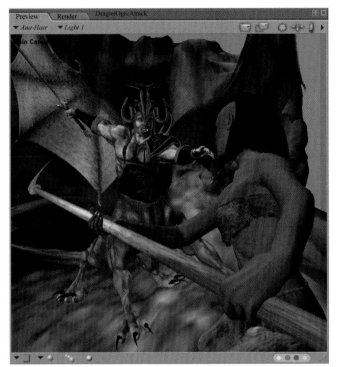

Figure 6.6 The female figure is more prominent in the final composition than in the sketch.

Figure 6.7 "Dragon Ogre Attack" final image.

Step-by-Step: Creating a Lifelike Model of Pinhead

Of the many considerations that went into developing a lifelike model of Pinhead, the most notable were the differences between the actual structure of the face of actor Doug Bradley and that which is visible after the final application of the Pinhead makeup and prosthetics.

1. In an effort to bring as much reality to the model and its expressions as possible, I utilize as many still and motion references of Doug without makeup as possible, as well as the obvious footage that can be obtained from the various *Hellraiser* films. The model is built to closely resemble Doug, with morph development attempting to capture his facial expressions as accurately as possible. See Figure 6.8.

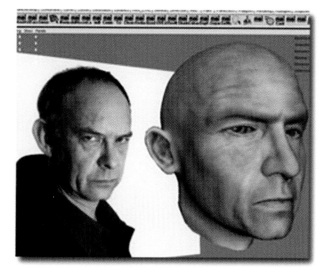

Figure 6.8 Use as many still and motion references as possible to create a sense of realism in the model.

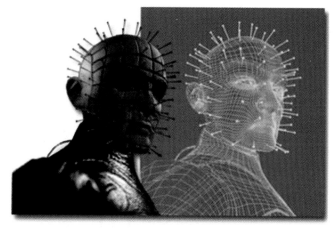

Figure 6.9 Model only the parts of the actor's body that show.

2. Now that the Doug model is complete, I need to do further morph sculpting to develop the look of the face to correspond with that of the final Pinhead makeup applications.

3. Because much of the costume is form-fitting leather, I save a great deal of polygon overhead by modeling only the parts of the actor's body that show rather than creating a full nude and then running calculation-intensive simulations for the leather over it. This approach allows me to create a lightweight figure that still maintains the look of the character while giving the maximum ease of use. I create two versions of the costume's skirt section at different levels of detail, both of which are designed for cloth simulation. See Figure 6.9.

4. One particularly challenging aspect of Pinhead is in defining the way in which the "pins" emerging from his head will be able to move along with the morphs of the face. Knowing that this will present some hurdles later in production, I develop much of the character's facial morphs using an extensive bone/muscle rig that drives the mesh of the face and guides the placement of the pins as the face moves. See Figure 6.10.

5. Next, I animate the rig through a long sequence of expressions to test the expressions and the way the pins react to them. Once I achieve a satisfactory result, I "bake" the animation's keyframes to morph targets for the head and pins.

6. Finally, I link these morph sets so that the animators need only one set of controls to drive the expression of the character and the pins simultaneously. See Figure 6.11.

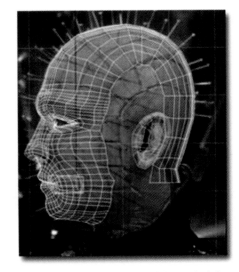

Figure 6.10 Define the movement of the pins by linking morph sets from a bone/muscle rig.

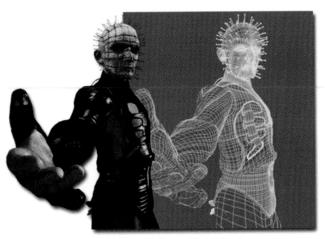

Figure 6.11 A lifelike model of Pinhead.

Insights

Lighting

Keylight, eyelight, fills, rims, and kickers. Understanding how real-world lighting works yields a thousand times better results from Poser, or any other 3D package for that matter. I keep a copy of *Lighting for Digital Video & Television* right on my desk. Aside from just biting the bullet and reading up on the technical aspects of lighting, it's important to think through the artistic uses of lighting. For that, I recommend *Dynamic Light and Shade*, an absolutely brilliant book from Burne Hogarth.

As far as my personal preferences on lighting, I'm a fan of horror, sci-fi, and film noir, so mood is always the principal goal of the lighting. I am accused of doing images that are too dark sometimes, and though I do try to illuminate a bit more than I used to, I'm not about to go flooding scenes with blaring bright white light! There's no mood in that! I want to see soft, diffuse shadows on the heroine's face and stark, monolithic shapes cast from a hero or a monster. I like a ton of contrast and for the shadows to really guide the eye. Just look at the *Sin City* books from Frank Miller and then the film version from Robert Rodriguez—it's the best treatment of light and shadow I think I've ever seen, and there's hardly any real detail showing in most of the imagery. Shapes are defined entirely by the light and darkness, and from it you get these simple, powerful, moody, iconic images.

As far as my personal use of Poser lighting, there's what I feel I *have* to do for product art, and then there's what I do for myself. For product art, it's all about even lighting and showing off the model. Frankly, I hate it, though it's a necessary evil. Users have to be able to "see" what they're buying, and I understand that, but I always feel like the "character" of the subject is lost when the lighting can't be used more sculpturally. For myself, well…

Scenes

One particularly handy technique, whether for Poser or any other 3D application, is to plan a scene in such a way as to set up the foreground, middle ground, and background so that they can be rendered separately and then composited later. The best way I know to do that in Poser is to bring all the elements into one scene where I work as though I'm going to render it all at once, but then when I'm finished working on it, I remove the foreground and mid-ground elements and save them as a separate file. I repeat the process to get different files for each pass of rendering and then render each of those files separately to some kind of image that holds the alpha channel, like TIF, PSD, or PNG. By separating the render process in this way, I save myself the pain of rerendering everything at once in the event I need a last-minute change.

Keyboard Commands

I know a couple of semi-undocumented keyboard commands for manipulating the camera directly in the viewport that help a lot. Hold down the Spacebar and click-drag in the viewport to pan. Hold down the Spacebar and Ctrl-click-drag to zoom. Selecting a camera or object and holding the Shift key while dragging in the viewport locks that selection and prevents anything else from moving.

TIP

The Selection Lock locks all objects in the scene. It's useful when posing hands because they have 16 individual elements that tend to get in the way of one another.

Q&A

What are some of your favorite Poser features?

The reason I have stuck with Poser for so many years—over 10 of them now—is the same today as it was when I started with it: I like the idea of the library system in the application. It's such a simple concept, but the way it's implemented in Poser is much more immediate and intuitive than anything I've seen remotely similar anywhere else. I've been modeling since before I started using Poser, so I've always had exhaustive numbers of my own models to use, but the way you can store them as props, develop models into figures, save out poses and animated poses… Yup, the library system is definitely the feature that makes Poser really valuable.

I continue to be pleased, since versions 5 and 6, with the implementation of procedural materials and shading networks. There's a lot more there than folks realize, and if it ever becomes Mental Ray or Renderman compliant, Poser will definitely jump to a whole new level in terms of the work that is produced with it. The new animation layers function of Poser 7 shows a lot of promise, too. I could see that, as time goes on, becoming more and more of a feature that I'll use a lot.

How does Poser fit in your creative process and workflow?

Well, actually Poser is kind of the last in line for me most of the time now, though not because of any fault of its own. The work that we do at Sixus1 is really divided into two areas: modeling/animation for film and commercial clients, and development of content for the Poser users. For most of our work, we have a Maya-centric pipeline: All of our modeling is done in Maya, and most of our film and commercial-related clients' needs end up going in that direction as well. Where Poser comes in for us is often in the case of doing animatics and blocking to help work out the previsualization of some film or animation we are about to start work on. Once again, it's the whole library thing: We can pop all manner of stuff into our scene from the library and get some fast visual feedback on everything from the best placement of props and actor blocking to ideas on how best to plan out our camera movements.

Previsualization is definitely an area where Poser is handy in a production environment. We do get some opportunities to render out of Poser as we're putting together the test art and promotional art for Poser content, and I still like to take a bit of time here and there to work with a monster or two from our libraries.

How do you use the lighting tools in Poser?

The first thing I do anytime I'm working on an image for myself out of Poser is delete every light in the scene and start with a single point light or spotlight, usually set to pure white with shadows set for raytracing. Then I move that light to wherever seems appropriate based on whatever lighting ideas I've come up with in my thumbnail sketches (there it is again: draw, draw, draw!) and do some low-res testing to see how the shapes in the scene are accented by that single light. From there, I add in one or two other lights, usually spotlights with low shadow map settings for a super-soft shadow, keeping their intensity as low as I can get away with. Once I'm comfortable with the level of illumination that gives, I start manipulating the colors of the lights until the image conveys the atmospheric and emotional mood I'm after.

Occasionally, if things are close to what I want but seem just a touch too dark, I might throw in one or two infinite lights with their shadow casting turned off and their intensity set very, very low. This is a quick and dirty way to emulate ambient lighting in Poser, but I have to be careful with it because it can make the scene look washed out.

I know a lot of users out there are really into using massive light sets and tons upon tons of spotlights, but that just doesn't work for me. I like to keep my lighting as simple as possible and use it to convey mood and shape. The more lights there are in the scene, the more management is required, the longer the render times get, and the harder it is to control the color and shadow of the scene, so I try to keep lighting as simple as possible.

What advice do you have for artists who are starting out with Poser?

Draw thumbnails first. Save often. Shove as much RAM in the machine as possible. Don't let the program fool you. There's more to creating artwork than just loading a figure, slapping on a pose, picking out a neat prop or two, tossing in a light set, and clicking the Render button. I'm going to say it again now: Draw, draw, draw! Even if you think you completely blow chunks at drawing, do it. Stick figures, silly little chicken scratches—anything! Just do it.

If you think through what you are trying to create before you sit down with the program, you will be many steps ahead of the game. Sure, sometimes it can be fun to go trolling through libraries of content thinking, "hmmm… maybe a little of this and a little of that," but I find that the best work comes when you start with a blank page. One of the most powerful aspects of Poser, the libraries, can also become a real hindrance to an aspiring artist. It can be easy for people to think only in terms of the limits of what is in their runtime rather than just cutting loose their imagination and seeing where it leads.

Recognize Poser for what it is: a tool. A really good artist doesn't have a favorite brush but rather has an array of brushes he'll use to achieve an end result. Rule the tool; don't let the tool rule you.

Where do you think computer-generated imagery will be 5–10 years from now?

My guess is that eventually the continued trend of technology pricing and development will reach a point where render times will become less and less of an issue, although you still have to consider that every time the speed increases, we artists push hard for the tools to be able to do more. I guess people will still be swearing at their slow render times when they're pushing their 20 zillion poly scenes around with multilayer skin and muscle simulation. People are actually a little spoiled already. I remember how slow the machines were when I started, so hopefully I won't ever lose the appreciation of how fast things really are now.

Thinking on it, I would expect to eventually see some new paradigm in modeling that moves beyond the concept of tri- and quadrangulated polygons as everything is essentially based on now and into some form of procedural that has inherent dynamics and physics generated from underlying mathematics as opposed to polygonal surface approximation. Five years ago, NURBS modeling was "it." It was "bleeding edge" because of the math, and you could get resolution independence. But in the end, the models still translated out to polygons. I expect to see something that possibly treats 3D as a virtually infinite point cloud, where every point in space can be allocated to systems of math that emulate physics in a much more realistic way than we can foresee now.

What I think the future will hold for artists using digital media is kind of a blessing and a curse: We'll be able to do anything. We virtually can now, but just what will we do with that much power? Will we tell better stories, or will we just tell a lot more really bad ones but with great resolution and realism?

LES GARNER

Studio

Software: Poser, Maya, Photoshop, ZBrush, Premiere, After Effects, Vue Infinite

Hardware: 12 networked machines (most running Athlon 64 processors with 2 Gigs of RAM minimum) 8×9 Wacom Intuos 3, 10×12 Intuos 2, a widescreen Gateway monitor via KVM switching; much of the rig does double duty for both video and audio production

Contact
Sixus1 Media, LLC ■ Cincinnati, OH ■
http://www.sixus1media.com

PHIL COOKE

About the Artist

Phil is a self-taught artist who was born in Essex, England and studied environmental engineering. He is considered a Poser content creation expert. He lives with his wife Jan in Lawrenceburg, Kentucky. Together, they have 7 children, 11 grandchildren, and 8 great grandchildren. He works full time on creating content, is active with his church, and works on Habitat for Humanity and other community-oriented projects.

Artist's Statement

Early in my professional career, I would produce top-quality engineering drawings, but the moment anything freehand or "arty" was required, in all honesty a kid with a box of Crayolas would do better than me. I could see it in my head, but I could not get it to flow out of a pencil. I became involved in computer graphics primarily because most of the programs came with an undo command. Undo gave me a chance to actually get somewhere without the frustration of continually erasing through the paper.

I was once given an IQ test that said I had excellent spatial awareness. I'm thinking, "Well, I'd better have, or I'm going to be out of pocket to the tune of one length of pipe if it does not align to the bottom of the cistern after bending it through six right angles!" I can think in 3D, which is probably something I was born with. Who knows? But it sure comes in handy when it comes to making 3D computer models.

Did using a computer to create art come naturally? Was it easy? No way! However, I wasn't going to let a small gray box that my kids used to play games on get the better of me. I was just too stubborn to give up. And if I can do this stuff, anyone can.

Influences

I basically do this for fun. It exercises the gray matter certainly, but if it were not fun, I'd be doing something else. I enjoy the interaction with other Poser users via the online forums. I think it's great that we can all learn from each other.

"Mermaids."

Techniques

The Creative Process

I get some ideas from here, some from over there, and one or two from under this. I tend to think sideways, not in straight lines. A train of thought quickly gets derailed, and I end up paddling my bicycle without a parachute.

Poser is my primary 3D manipulation tool. I might create a figure in trueSpace but animate and render it in Poser. I love the Cloth room. I enjoy making spider webs with the nodes in the Material room. The Poser animation suite is about the only one I have had any success with.

Although Poser does indeed come with a wealth of content, I spend most of my time creating my own new models and figures. I enjoy the challenge.

Step-by-Step Tutorial: How to Make a Mermaid

There are several ways to make a mermaid. For this example, I use the e frontier Terai Yuki 2 figure and seamlessly attach a tail to her.

1. Starting with Figure 7.1, I load the Terai Yuki figure into the scene and set her in a zero pose. Next, I bring her legs together as if they are to be the tail. Then I import a cylinder. This cylinder was created in the 3D modeling application trueSpace.

2. Now, using one of the Python scripts I wrote, I'm able to shrink-wrap the cylinder to the Terai Yuki figure. See Figure 7.2.

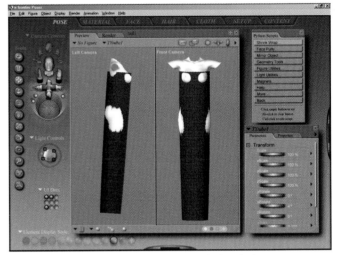

Figure 7.1 Place the figure inside the cylinder.

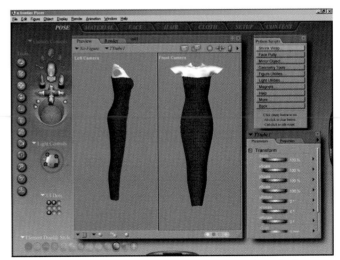

Figure 7.2 Use a Python script to shrink-wrap the cylinder to the figure.

TIP

Don't be put off from using Poser Python scripts. In the same way that you do not need to know anything about computer programming to be able to use a Windows application, you do not need to know anything about Python to be able to use these scripts. The Shrink Wrap script used here is part of my Poser Tool Box. It is set up so that all you need to do is click a button. It is available from http://www.philc.net/PoserToolBox.htm.

3. With the tail section formed, I export it into trueSpace and edit the abdomen area so that it exactly meets up with the existing Terai Yuki chest. See Figure 7.3.

4. I then extend the lower portion to form the flukes. Once completed, I import it again into Poser. See Figure 7.4.

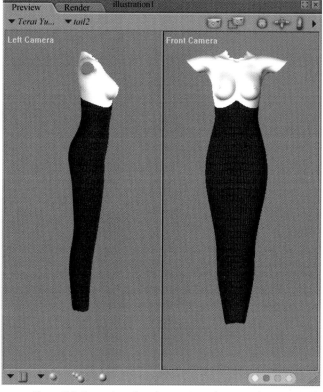

Figure 7.3 Export the tail section to a 3D authoring application. This example uses trueSpace.

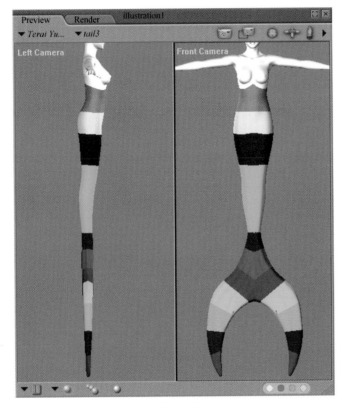

Figure 7.4 Form the flukes. Color-coding keeps groups organized.

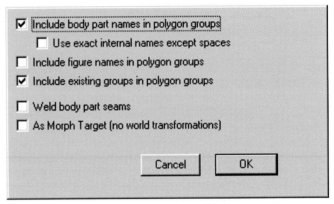

Figure 7.5 Export Options dialog box.

5. I color-code the sections to facilitate the tail being split into groups later. Then I can export the required Terai Yuki body parts and the tail as a single object. My selected export options are shown in Figure 7.5.

6. The existing body already has its groups defined, so the next process is to define the groups in the tail. I can do this with the Grouping tool in the Poser Setup room, but my preference is to use an application called UVMapper (http://www.uvmapper.com). See Figure 7.6.

7. In UVMapper, I select my material and assign it to a group. With that done and still in UVMapper, I assign the model's finalized materials and create its UV map. The UV map defines the way in which the texture is applied to the model. It is a bit like peeling a banana and then laying the skin flat so that you can paint it yellow.

Figure 7.7 is part of the mermaid's UV map. I'll use this later as a template when I create the textures.

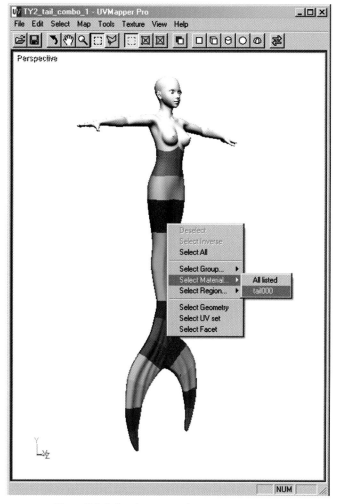

Figure 7.6 Define the groups using Poser or UVMapper.

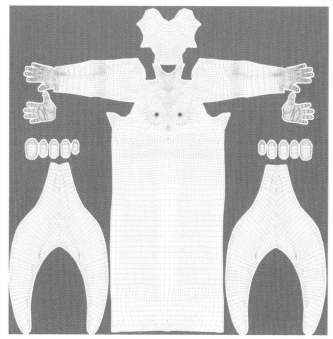

Figure 7.7 The mermaid's UV map.

TIP

Using symmetry is a great time saver. For example, the mermaid uses a left/right body part naming convention—lFluke1, rFluke1 and lFluke2, rFluke2, and so on. This enables me to use the Poser symmetry command. I'll only need to set up the joints in one-half of the model and then apply symmetry to mirror the jointing to the other side. It's half the work and half the trouble.

To recap, at this stage I have the Terai Yuki torso, head, arms, and tail as a single 3D model. I save it in OBJ format to a Geometries folder within the Poser runtime. The next stage is to make it into a poseable figure. I could either take the model into the Poser Setup room and create a bone system, or I could write a hierarchy file. For this example, I'm going to go the hierarchy route.

A child can have only one parent. Consider a humanoid figure. The two thighs adjoin the hip; they do not touch each other. It's the same with the left and right flukes. They adjoin the base of the tail and do not touch.

A hierarchy file defines the child/parent relationship between body parts. It also sets the axes of rotation. Getting the axes of rotation right is not important—*it's essential!* What does it mean?

8. The P4 man in Figure 7.8 has a forearm that can rotate in three directions. Admittedly, this is one direction more than most humans and probably explains the poor man's expression; however, it serves the purpose.

So for the forearm here, the first order of rotation is "X." You can see the hierarchy text for the mermaid in Listing 7.1 and on the enclosed DVD. If you look closely, there is an exception to every rule. Here the exception is in the feet. They need to twist along the length of the shin and not toward the toes. Please read the sidebar beside Listing 7.1; it explains the hierarchy text line by line.

Figure 7.8 The axes of rotation.

TIP

Golden Rule: The first order of rotation, usually referred to as *twist*, is axial to the body part.

Listing 7.1

```
objFile :Runtime:Geometries:TeraiYuki
2:TY2mermaid.obj
1 hip yxz
   2 abdomen yzx
      3 chest yzx
         4 neck yzx
            5 head yzx
               6 rEye xyz
               6 lEye xyz
         4 rCollar xyz
            5 rShldr xyz
               6 rForeArm xyz
                  7 rHand xyz
                     8 rThumb1 xyz
                        9 rThumb2 xyz
                           10 rThumb3 xyz
                     8 rIndex1 xyz
                        9 rIndex2 xyz
                           10 rIndex3 xyz
                     8 rMid1 xyz
                        9 rMid2 xyz
                           10 rMid3 xyz
                     8 rRing1 xyz
                        9 rRing2 xyz
                           10 rRing3 xyz
                     8 rPinky1 xyz
                        9 rPinky2 xyz
                           10 rPinky3 xyz
         4 lCollar xyz
            5 lShldr xyz
               6 lForeArm xyz
                  7 lHand xyz
                     8 lThumb1 xyz
                        9 lThumb2 xyz
                           10 lThumb3 xyz
```

Hierarchy Text
An Explanation of What Each Line Means

```
objFile :Runtime:Geometries:TeraiYuki
2:TY2mermaid.obj
```

The first line states where the geometry file is located. It is usually within the Runtime:Geometry directories. The directory delimiter : (colon) is used in preference to the more usual \ (backslash) so that it is both PC and Mac compatible.

```
1 hip yxz
   2 abdomen yzx
      3 chest yzx
            etc
```

The code reads as follows:

The chest is a child of the abdomen, which is in turn a child of the hip. The line indent is unimportant; it is only there to make it easier for humans to see the relationship between body parts. Poser reads the hierarchy level number—that is, 1 for the hip, 2 for the abdomen, 3 for the chest, and so on.

After each body part, you see "YZX, XYZ, ZYX" and so on. These are the rotation orders. Remember the golden rule? The first order of rotation must be axial to the body part. So for the torso, neck, and head, it will be YZX. For the arms, it will be XYZ, and for the tail, it will be YZX. The order of the second and third rotations is less important. Generally, whichever rotation is bent most should go last. So a shin would be YZX. It's best to match right and left sides.

Listing 7.1 *(continued)*

```
                8 lIndex1 xyz
                 9 lIndex2 xyz
                    10 lIndex3 xyz
                8 lMid1 xyz
                 9 lMid2 xyz
                    10 lMid3 xyz
                8 lRing1 xyz
                 9 lRing2 xyz
                    10 lRing3 xyz
                8 lPinky1 xyz
                 9 lPinky2 xyz
                    10 lPinky3 xyz

  2 Thighs yzx
    3 Shins yzx
      4 Ankles yzx
        5 Feet yzx
          6 Fluke yzx
            7 rFluke1 yzx
              8 rFluke2 yzx
                9 rFluke3 yzx
                  10 rFluke4 yzx
            7 lFluke1 yzx
              8 lFluke2 yzx
                9 lFluke3 yzx
                  10 lFluke4 yzx
ikChain tail Thighs Shins Feet Ankles Fluke
ikChain right-arm rShldr rForeArm rHand
ikChain left-arm lShldr lForeArm lHand
```

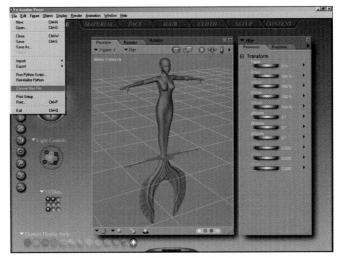

Figure 7.9 Convert the hierarchy file into the Poser figure.

9. The moment of truth comes in Figure 7.9 when I create the figure in Poser. I do this by using the menu command File, Convert Hier File. I don't worry about the colors; they simply have not been set yet. I save the figure to the library.

10. For fun, I can set up all the joints either from scratch, or with a little skullduggery, I can copy some of the joint details from the original Terai Yuki figure. The figure's CR2 files are just big text files and can be edited in any text editor. There are also a number of Poser file editors available; the one I use is Cr2 Editor by John Stallings. Using this editor, I copy and paste the joint sections from the original figure into the new mermaid. See Figure 7.10.

NOTE

The order of rotation for the abdomen is the same for both figures. This ensures that we do not run into problems with the abdomen/hip joints. The hip is not copied over because the new hip has tail groups below it rather than buttocks.

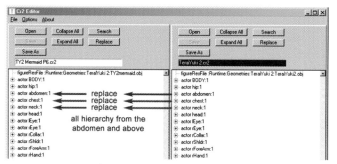

Figure 7.10 Cr2, a Poser file editor.

11. In Figure 7.11, I copy the materials from the original figure into the mermaid. The order in which they are listed is unimportant. I still need to set up the materials for the new tail, but this saves setting up the materials in the "human" areas, which use the original Terai Yuki textures. After copying the materials and saving the figure to the library, I reload the mermaid figure into the Poser scene by double-clicking on its thumbnail. The next task is to set up the joint parameters in the new tail.

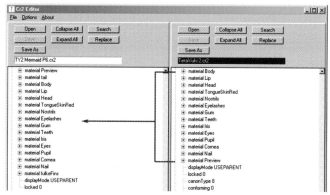

Figure 7.11 Copy and paste the joint sections.

12. Although the abdomen joints are copied from the original figure, the hip also contains abdomen-related joint information. To force Poser to update this data, I select the abdomen and use the Poser menu command Window, Joint Editor to open the Joint Editor window displayed on the left in Figure 7.12.

The top section of the Joint Editor has a drop-down list giving access to each joint. Here the Z rotate (side-to-side) joint is shown. To force Poser to update the hip, I need to make a slight change in the joint parameter settings. I can toggle the Spherical Falloff Zones on and off or change the joint angles slightly.

TIP

Setting up joint parameters can be a bit daunting. They were for me at first, so I prepared two onscreen videos explaining how they work. You can find them in my chapter on the DVD that is included with this book.

13. Now that the joints are complete, the next task is to complete setting up the material. The skin areas are already taken care of, but I need to address the tail. For this, I use the Material room shown in Figure 7.13.

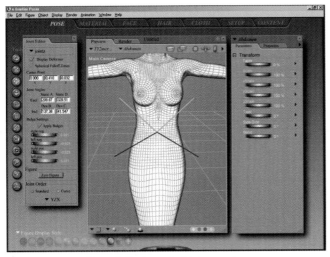

Figure 7.12 Set up the joint parameters.

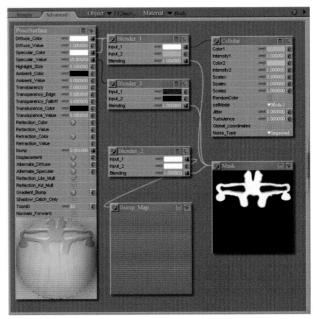

Figure 7.13 The Poser Material room.

I want to give the illusion that the mermaid's scales blend into her human skin. I also want to be able to easily change the color and highlight of the scales. The Poser 6 material node system allows me to do this relatively easily. I select the mermaid's body material. Referring to Figure 7.13, I'll explain each element:

- **Mask**—This is probably the key element in this setup. It is a black-and-white image that allows me to separate different areas of the model's surface. I create it in Photoshop using the mermaid's UV map as a template.

- **Bump Map**—This is a grayscale image with a repetitive fish scale pattern.

- **Cellular**—This is one of the available Material nodes. It is accessed by right-clicking in a free area and then selecting New Node, 3D Textures, Cellular. It uses the two selected colors to create a variegated pattern.

- **Blender 1**—Input 1 influences the white areas of the mask. Input 2 influences the black areas of the mask. I define the color of input 2 by point-sampling the mermaid's skin color at the base of the neck. Then I plug the output from the blender into Diffuse and Specular colors, which provides the primary component of this material.

- **Blender 2**—This blends the grayscale fish scales with the mask and plugs into the bump node. All the black areas of the mask then render bumpy, and the white areas render smooth.

- **Blender 3**—Here I want just the scales to have a blue sheen. The mask enables me to exclude the skin areas.

- **Poser Surface**—This is the summation of all the nodes. The result is shown in its lower panel.

NOTE

Many of the effects are not evident in the preview window until the image is rendered. Ensure that the render settings are set to take advantage of the parameters.

---

14. I put the mermaid together with some hair and extra fins. I render it, resulting in the finished mermaid in Figure 7.14.

15. By changing some node colors, I can quickly obtain variations such as Figures 7.15 and 7.16. I can't decide which mermaid is my favorite!

Figure 7.14 The finished mermaid.

16. For a totally different approach to the Poser bone system, see Figure 7.17, which is also included on the DVD that accompanies this book.

Figure 7.15 Try changing the node color.

Figure 7.16 Another beautiful finished piece.

Figure 7.17 Gladys: a free Poser figure included on the DVD.

Resources

On the DVD

- Gladys—Free Poser figure
- Terai Yuki 2 Free Mermaid figure
- Joint Parameters—Onscreen video tutorial
- Set Up Room—Onscreen video tutorial
- Add Body Handle— HTML file
- Joint Parameters—HTML file

Links

- http://www.philc.net/PoserToolBox.htm
- http://www.contentparadise.com
- http://www.renderosity.com

PHIL COOKE

Studio

Software: Poser, trueSpace, Photoshop, UVMapper, Deep Exploration

Hardware: I contacted Gateway and told them exactly what I wanted and what my budget was. They sold me a gray box and two flat-screen monitors. It all works—that's all I know!

Contact

Phil Cooke ■ PhilC Designs Ltd ■ pcooke@philc.net ■ http://www.philc.net

PHIL COOKE

AS SHANIM AND SILIPHIEL

About the Artists

Aery Soul is composed of As Shanim and Siliphiel. We share every part of our life and get along well. We're passionate about our work, which offers us the chance to express ourselves. We always try to do our best and improve our skills.

We started producing Poser content more than five years ago, and since then, we've been Renderosity Merchant of the Year. We're still enjoying it and have a long list of projects we want to create.

Artists' Statement

As content developers, we try to push Poser limits and exploit all its features. We strive to offer people something that we consider a tool for further enjoying Poser and its features and give form to their imagination and art rather than simple products to be used as they are. Our creations usually require some work on the part of the user to be exploited to their fullest but, as in every field, this is unavoidable if you want to achieve a higher level of scene and imagery creation.

Our favorite genres to create Poser material for are fantasy, sci-fi, and post-apocalyptic. We don't disregard other genres, but we feel that these three allow us to be the most creative.

In 2001, we wanted to construct a comic but couldn't find enough material for it. That's why we decided to tackle the creation of Poser clothes, scenarios, and poses ourselves. In the end, we didn't make the comic, but we continued creating Poser content and are still enjoying doing it because we like to express ourselves through it.

Dynamism is one of the key words of our work. Hair, clothes, and people move, and we want to get rid of that static, marionette feeling that many Poser images have and turn it into something dynamic and natural.

For our own work, either for promotional or personal purposes, we try to achieve the best result possible within Poser, exploiting its main features: the Material room, IBL; ambient occlusion, and the FireFly render options. All these elements need to be taken into consideration because all of them contribute to a good final rendering. Of course, some post work is always necessary both for correcting imperfections (joints, poke-through, and so on) and for adding details and effects that are difficult or impossible to add in Poser.

Influences

We admire the work of several artists, including Masamune Shirow, Brom, and Luis Royo. Video games, comics, and role-playing games also inspire us for both the games and content and the respective artworks. Some of our favorites include the *Final Fantasy* series, *Warhammer, Heroes of Might*, and *Magic*. And, of course, we look at 3D galleries to study lighting and scene building techniques and to improve our own renders.

"Bright Heart of the Forest."

Techniques

The Creative Process

We work in Poser during the whole creation process since our work needs to be used in Poser. That's why at every stage of development, we check whether everything behaves well within the program.

The secret to creating good images within Poser can be summed up in one word: patience.

Posing the character, adding some preset props, and pressing the render key combination to create a result in 5 minutes rarely leads to an eye-catching and telling image.

Those artists who are admired for their 3D images usually spend weeks creating their masterpieces, and much of this time is spent with the various tools at their disposal. They start with a pencil sketch, pose the models, render with their 3D tool of choice (Maya, 3ds Max, LightWave, and so on), and then add effects in post work with a 2D editing program such as Photoshop, Painter, or Paint Shop Pro.

One of Poser's strengths is as a previsualization and reference tool. The various characters in the scene can be modified easily. Thanks to all the content created by third parties, a Poser user does not need to have modeling skill. He can just focus on the scene setup.

Poser offers the user great flexibility in posing characters and clothes. It is easy and quick to change a pose, an expression, or anything else on a character. Also, because of the wide content base of clothes, characters, sceneries, and so on that is available, the possibilities are endless for letting your imagination loose and really creating something to be proud of.

The Poser 6 FireFly render engine can certainly render good images with a satisfactory speed. You might think that it's better to produce a quick render rather than a better, slower one since you can add details and contrasts in post work, but the best way to create a good 3D image is to choose the most advanced options and exploit what the program can offer. This means that when the post work stage comes, you'll have the pleasure of working with an image that is already detailed and complete on its own and certainly easier to enhance.

Drawing details on a 3D piece by hand is not easy because most of the time the difference between the 3D and the 2D part is such that the image looks messy and not very charming. We are more interested in post work that enhances our 3D render and concerns color tones, character joint correction, and final image composition. The following tutorial focuses on posing the various characters and setting the lights. Those are both important parts of creating a good 3D image.

Step-by-Step Tutorial: Creating "Parking Trouble"

We create the image "Parking Trouble" (see Figure 8.1) by combining four renders done in Poser: the background "Urban Sci-Fi Set" by Stonemason, "the droid" (Dystopian droid by Stonemason e Moebius), "the car" (City Car by Stonemason), and the character with all clothing and accessories ("carattere e clothes" by Aery Soul). We prefer to render the various figures in four different steps because it gives us more control over every element during the post work stage.

1. First, we set up the various elements of the scene and then the lights. We save the complete scene and then continually delete anything we don't need to render.

> ## NOTE
>
> We don't do post work on the separate elements of the image. We do all post work on the composition of the final image.

Figure 8.1 "Parking Trouble" complete scene.

Figure 8.2 "Ivy" is the focus of the composition.

2. Figure 8.2 shows the final Poser render. The female character is the focus of the image. She is responding to the droid in a determined way since her car can stay where she parked it. Therefore, we make both her pose and expression convey the idea of determination. We fine-tune these elements and then give her some clothes. We choose various clothing pieces and come up with a sort of "space-chick" who is proud and self-confident with impressive and cyber metal gloves. This part takes a long time because we have so many options. We choose the result mainly because of personal taste. We apply the skin shader to the character and then render her.

3. In Figure 8.3, we choose five different lights for our scene and set them as follows:

   a. We begin with an IBL and set the Ambient Occlusion strength to 0.5. In the Color node, we connect the image of a gray sphere, lightened in the center. We set the light intensity at 60 percent and make the color a red tint (R=1.000, G=0.980, B=0.980). The light position has no importance; it doesn't cast shadows.

   b. Next, we adjust the spotlight on the left. This light strongly illuminates the contour of the right part of our character.

c. For Specular Light, we set the light diffuse color to zero (color set to black) in the material settings. This means that this light will only act upon the specularity of the objects in the scene, making, for example, metals more bright and enhancing the outer curves of the character's shape.

d. We set Infinite Light at 50 percent intensity. It casts shadows with the depth map shadow set to 0.500 (quite weak). This light is especially useful for the character skin, to enhance the subsurface scatter (SSS.) This light color is red/orange (a sort of sun).

e. The spotlight with raytracing shadow is the light that simulates the sky. We set it at an intensity of 75 percent and set the color to be sky blue. We set the shadow parameter to 2, so the shadow is quite strong. This shadow, from an artistic viewpoint, is useful to give depth and thickness to the clothes the character is wearing; note, for example, the shadow of the pendant on the character's shirt.

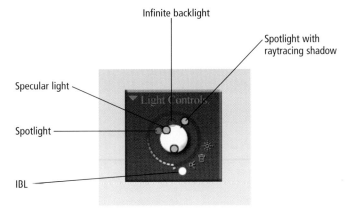

Figure 8.3 Five different lights are used for this image.

4. The other elements in the scene are simpler. We don't need to move the elements because we did the scene composition in step 1. Using the same lights that we used for the female character, we render the other three elements (see Figures 8.4, 8.5, and 8.6). When saving the image from Poser, we always choose PSD format or any other format that retains the alpha channel.

TIP

We make no aim toward realism in the light settings; instead, our artistic research aims for a result that is pleasant and gratifying. We use the violent light from the side and the strong shadow to give depth and weight to the character. Any light setting can be the right one if the light is pleasant to the eye and it achieves the goal you are aiming for.

TIP

Images in Poser are usually rendered over a white background. Rendering over black instead of white helps to reduce or eliminate the white halo that usually remains around the image. The neutral tone will be less apparent, and because Poser's alpha channel is premultiplied, it will be better antialiased.

5. At this point, Poser has done its part, and we're ready to assemble the image. We open the images in Photoshop and cut out any remaining white/transparency via the alpha channel to get rid of any remaining white "halo." (Ctrl-click the alpha channel for a clear selection.) We select Layer, Matting, Remove White Matte.

Figure 8.4 The car element is "City Car" by Stonemason.

Figure 8.6 The urban scene is "Urban Sci-Fi Set" by Stonemason.

6. Next, we imagine that the image is composed on four different levels. The female character and the droid occupy the first level, or the foreground. The second level is just behind them, by the car. The third is in the background, by the sci-fi building. The fourth is the infinite background, by the sky.

Figure 8.5 The droid element is "Dystopian droid" by Stonemason e Moebius.

AS SHANIM AND SILIPHIEL

7. We start with the post work done on the sci-fi building.

In Figure 8.7, we apply a subtle Gaussian blur. We choose the blur value based on the result we are aiming for. We could blur the background so much that no detail is noticeable anymore. In this case, because the building is not too far away, the blurring is minimal. We also create a black-and-white gradient, which makes the top part lighter and the bottom darker. By contrast, we could also make the bottom part lighter and the top darker if the sky were dark or if we wanted to draw more attention to the bottom part of the image. For the gradient layer, we set the Blending option to Color Dodge at 12 percent opacity. The most important thing is to try different options.

> ## NOTE
>
> The original building render is cold and detailed, like a 3D render. Our objective is to make it warmer. Also, it should give the idea that it stays in the distance and that its colors match on the top with the sky's color that we are putting behind it as the fourth level of our composition. A quick and effective method to achieve this effect is slightly blurring the image and desaturating the colors. In this case, we have a sunny day with a blue sky, giving it a sky-blue nuance.

8. We want to give our building a sky-blue nuance and more dynamic and creative colors. In Figure 8.8, we duplicate the building layer, name it Blue, desaturate the image until it is gray, and recolor it sky blue. Now we use the Gaussian blur again.

Figure 8.7 Apply the Guassian blur.

Figure 8.8 Create dynamic colors with a duplicate layer.

9. We set the layer we named Blue to Linear Light at 15 percent opacity. See Figure 8.9.

Figure 8.9 Set Linear Light to 15 percent opacity.

Figure 8.10 Create depth using the eraser on a duplicate layer.

10. In Figure 8.10, we want to make the top of the building even bluer to give it a better sense of depth. We duplicate the Blue layer and, with the Eraser tool, we erase the lower part until we achieve the effect we want. In this case, we erase about three-fourths of the image.

11. We decide to create fake lights in Photoshop to make the image more interesting. In the following process, we enhance the red and yellow lights and make some metal parts brighter.

   a. We create a new layer named Aura.

   b. We select the Brush tool and set Opacity to 1 percent. The size of the brush determines the size of the light aura.

   c. We draw over the 7 (and over any other source of light/neon). That applies the effect to the Aura layer, as shown in Figure 8.11.

   d. We create a different aura layer for each different light color (red, yellow, and blue), which creates the aura effect every time we draw an invisible line.

12. In Figure 8.12, we add the car. We do a bit of post work on it because some textures don't look perfectly seamless. We cut off the car's glass and put it on a new layer that we set to Multiply 100 percent. Moreover, we add a subtle Gaussian blur.

Figure 8.11 Creating an aura using Photoshop.

Figure 8.12 Adding the car to the scene.

13. In Figure 8.13, we add the main characters: Ivy (our star) and the droid. The layer hierarchy corresponds to the tutorial, so Ivy and the droid become the top layers. We don't do any particular effect or post work on either of them. We do some minor correction on the droid, but Ivy and her clothes are exactly as they came out of Poser. We add to both layers a subtle sky-blue halo (Layer Style, Outer Glow, set on Screen at 25 percent opacity); this gives more focus to the main characters and simulates a halo of light reflected by the metal and the skin. We could perform a color adjustment on Ivy using the Selective Color function (Image, Adjustment, Selective Color) to enhance the color nuances of skin and clothes.

Figure 8.13 Add the main characters and Outer Glow.

14. As we did in step 11 with the background, in Figure 8.14, we add some reflection to the metal parts of the droid and to Ivy's arms.

15. We create a sort of atmosphere in a simple and effective way by overlaying a blurred image over our own image. We use an image that lacks strong color contrasts but has some nuance contrast. Usually it is a photograph or CG image of a landscape or sky. At this stage, it's nice to experiment with different pictures to see the various effects possible.

16. We blur this atmosphere image with Gaussian blur to get rid of all the details and to retain only the nuances of the image. We set the blending mode to Overlay and the Opacity value to 25 percent. Generally speaking, this atmosphere image should be the same as the infinite background—in this case, the sky—to create a more homogeneous look. We apply a brown/sky-blue gradient, with sky blue on the top and dark brown on the bottom. We set the blending mode of this layer as Overlay at 15 percent. See Figure 8.15.

17. The last step is adding the sky. We use an ordinary sky, set it as the first layer (on the bottom), and adjust its colors to match the scene. We delete the white upper part of the image (where we want our sky to be) through the selection of the alpha channel. Figure 8.16 shows the final image.

Figure 8.14 Add reflection to the metal elements of the characters.

Figure 8.15 Create atmosphere with a secondary image.

AS SHANIM AND SILIPHIEL

Figure 8.16 "Parking Trouble" final image.

Insights

Rendering

Often, we prefer the speed of the Poser 4 render engine to the better quality but slower FireFly engine. For a test render or when we need to look at some rendered detail, using the Poser 4 rendering engine can save some time. When the scene is ready for the final render, the FireFly engine is the only one to consider. In fact, the difference between the qualities of the two rendering engines is huge, and the image clearly shows it. The FireFly engine actually isn't very fast, compared to other 3D rendering tools, but the outcome is beautiful because it exploits the Material room and is quite customizable. See Figure 8.17 for a comparison of the two engines.

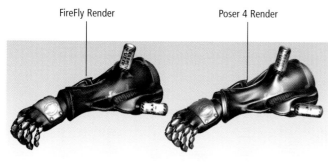

FireFly Render   Poser 4 Render

Figure 8.17 Rendering differences: FireFly versus Poser.

Material Room

One of Poser's most important features is certainly the Material room. By working with the Shader nodes, it is possible to completely modify the rendered output of a 3D object, making it look solid and realistic. Following are four examples that show the importance of the Material room. These methods are important steps in the realization of 3D images because they exploit typical Poser features and let us understand its rich features and potential.

> **NOTE**
>
> The difference in time between the two renders in the following examples is so small that it does not noticeably influence the speed of the final render. However, as we have noted, there is a telling difference in the quality of the outcome.

Both renders in Figure 8.19 were created using the render settings shown in Figure 8.18.

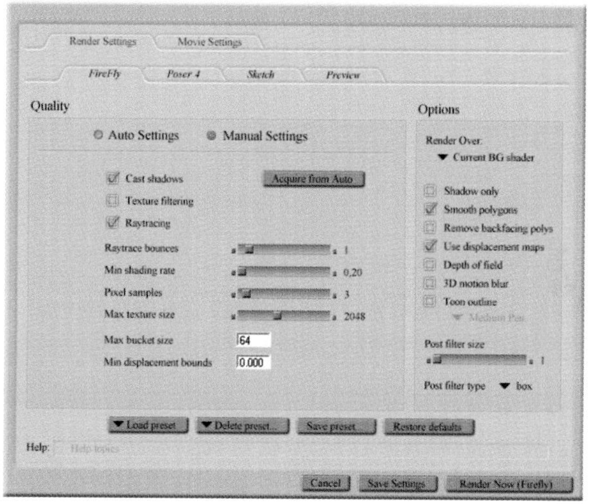

Figure 8.18 Manual render settings for FireFly.

In Figure 8.19, we did the render on the left using the shader settings included with the product ("Hanyma" by Aery Soul). In the render on the right, we simply connected the texture to the diffuse color. What we changed were the Material room settings.

The differences between the two images are immediately clear. We rendered both with the same light and render setting, but the second doesn't have the shader setup of the first. The shader is important because it enhances the leather folds, the metal parts, and the roughness of the fabric.

With Nodes   Without Nodes

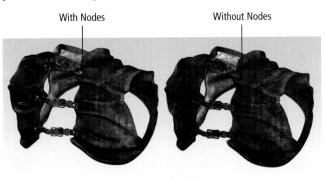

Figure 8.19 Nodes difference.

Figure 8.20 shows the various nodes set up in the Material room. Each has its own function. Utilizing the Material room features helps us to achieve better final renders using the FireFly engine, resulting in images that better represent our vision.

Complex Nodes   Simple Nodes

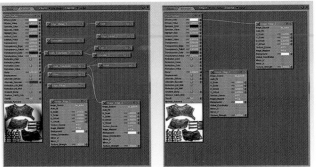

Figure 8.20 Nodes can be interconnected to create complex shaders, which allow more sophisticated simulation of surface properties.

Figure 8.21 illustrates how the Edge Blend math function renders the object as more solid and three-dimensional. To improve results, add at least the Edge Blend node to any object in a scene that doesn't have a proper shader.

With Edge Blend Node   Without Edge Blend Node

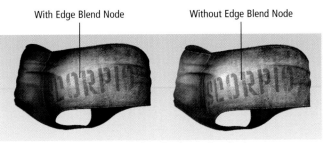

Figure 8.21 With and without Edge Blend.

Lighting

The lights are the most important feature for the outcome of an image.

There are numerous theories about light settings, each with its own merit. The choice of lights depends on the scene to be rendered.

We don't always need a tidy and well-defined shadow. The character doesn't always have to be perfectly lit from all directions. The number of lights usually varies from two to five, including the specular-only lights. The image-based lighting (IBL) is, generally speaking, useful in every setup, and its intensity can vary from 30 to 70 percent. It is typically connected to a texture map called a *light probe*, which is an image of an environment as reflected off a sphere.

You can use a directional light to enlighten a particular zone of the character and give more depth to the whole image. It is also useful for casting shadows. You can use a third backlight to create contrasts and, as far as the character skin is concerned, to enhance the subsurface scattering.

You can add more lights, for example, if you want to influence only the specular parts of the scene or to create a light contour.

Practice is the best teacher. You can find the ideal light for every occasion just by moving, adding, and modifying the lights of the scene. There is no perfect light setup, because every scene needs a fitting and custom lighting. A good light is one that makes sense with the scene and enhances its most important elements.

We try not to use too many lights in a scene so that the scene is simpler to work with and quicker to render. An IBL is necessary, even at low intensity, to add the global illumination. Ambient occlusion is also essential and works well with IBL. The rest depends on the actual scene.

Skin Shader

We spend a lot of time fine-tuning our characters' skin since it is a particular material. Poser helps us with the subsurface scatter (SSS) that tries to simulate the incidence of light on the human skin. The achievement of a good skin material is important for the outcome; otherwise, much of an image impact (especially when the characters are the image focus) is lost.

An add-on product for Poser (Realism Kits by Face_Off) allows automatic creation of a skin shader through a Python Script tool. The nodes that the program generates are complex, and customizing them is not intuitive, but the tool interface is rich with options. You can also find various free tutorials covering the creation of skin shaders. Those lead to simpler nodes settings but are much easier to customize and can still generate good-looking skin.

Q&A

What are some of your favorite Poser features?

We really like the Material room and the light and rendering options. Ambient Occlusion was a great addition—something that really adds to Poser's realism and outcome. Poser does justice to our hard work in creating clothes full of details and features.

Another feature we enjoy is Poser magnets, which are really useful and versatile tools. We include them in most of our products because they are helpful in controlling the flowing and moving of clothes or hair.

What advice do you have for artists who are starting out with Poser?

Scratch the surface. The Poser interface is intuitive, and the program includes a lot of content that you can load with the click of a few buttons and create something nice. However, if you really want to achieve something personal and original, if you really want to express yourself and give form to your inner worlds, you need to take some time to understand Poser and its various features. Exploiting those features in your work will pull your image's creation to a higher level.

What are some of your timesaving tips when using Poser on a project or artwork?

The area render is certainly a timesaver and an invaluable tool when creating content. You can quickly check the changes on a texture, on a morph, or when you need to alter a small scene and only need to rerender that part and then compose it in post work.

Being able to compare renders is also invaluable when you are working on something and need to see how things have actually changed.

As far as artworks are concerned, rendering scenes in different layers can certainly be useful.

Resources

On the DVD

- Artist Gallery

Links

- http://www.gfxartist.com/
- http://forums.cgsociety.org/
- http://www.ballisticpublishing.com/

AS SHANIM AND SILIPHIEL

Studio

Software: Poser, Maya, Photoshop, UV Mapper Pro
Hardware: For our working computers, we have 2 systems
with Conroe CPUs, each with 2GB memory and GeForce
video cards running on ASUS motherboards and plenty of
HD space; for rendering, we use 2 systems running AMDX2
CPUs with 2GB memory and GeForce video cards on
DFI motherboards; monitors are 21-inch Samsung,
17-inch Philips, 17-inch LG, and 19-inch Hyundai

Contact

As Shanim & Siliphiel of Aery Soul ■ Aery Soul Studio ■
Liguria, Italy ■ support@aerysoul.com ■ http://www.aerysoul.com

Gallery

"Totally Awesome."

CONTENT

"The Captain."

"Eclipse's Sorceress."

"Dreaming."

"Doubt."

"It Will Be Done."

"See No Evil."

"Another Mission."

"Yaara."

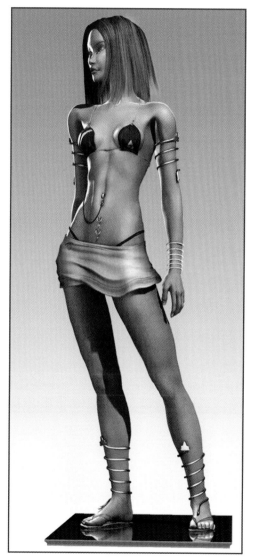

"Ivy."

TONY LUKE

About the Artist

Tony Luke was the first western writer (with Alan Grant) to script for the Japanese manga market with 1993's "Psychonauts." In 1994, he illustrated "Dominator" for Kodansha, which was the first original UK-created series to successfully break the Japanese market. He also boasts numerous collaborations with Glenn Fabry for Vertigo comics and Wildstorm, most notably the *Neverwhere* cover series.

Tony has directed many music videos that played on MTV. He originally formed Renga Media to oversee production of TV pilot *Archangel Thunderbird* for the Sci-Fi Channel in 1996. His first animated *Dominator* movie was released in 2003, followed by numerous short-form spin-offs and music videos. His new animated movie, *Dominator X*, is now in production.

Tony lives in Brighton, England with his wife Mandy and cat Poppy (aka The Official Renga Kitty).

Artist's Statement

The first hour I played around with Poser 3 back in 1999 was one of those magic watershed moments. I've been involved in what can broadly be called fantasy arts since I was just out of diapers, and though I'm now tipping toward the big 4-0, I still get a blast from all this. Call it a rush. It makes me feel like a kid again.

I set up Renga Media with Alan Grant to produce shows based on our creations. We were quickly joined by Doug Bradley (Pinhead from the *Hellraiser* movies, and our main voice actor) and producer Simon Moorhead, whose most recent work is the Neil Gaiman/Dave McKean film fantasy *Mirrormask*.

I love my job. And I still get a rush from time to time, particularly upon the completion of a piece of art or animation that's really pushed my working boundaries. And the best thing about Poser? It allows me to get something set up and animated quickly, while the idea's fresh. Cheers, guys, for helping this particular comic artist see his creations moving around onscreen.

Influences

I have had several important influences at different times of life, including *King Kong vs. Godzilla* at age 6 and *Star Wars* at age 11. I have also been influenced by all of Go Nagai's manga and anime, particularly *Devilman, Mazinger Z*, and *Mao Dante*; the art and design of Yasushi Nirasawa, Yoshitaka Amano, and Leiji Matsumoto; and the stories of Clive Barker, H. P. Lovecraft, and Graham Masterton.

"Dominator."

MOTION GRAPHICS

Techniques

The Creative Process

These days, most of the characters are locked down on paper long before they're built in Poser. But some mornings (very early mornings, if I've got insomnia), I like to "doodle" up a character straight from the runtime library, a folder that currently sits at 30GB on Renga Media's main hard drive; I've been collecting hairstyles, poses, and character bases since first venturing into Poser's crystal waters.

Essentially, once the character has been built (and lately, Renga Media is fortunate to have the very talented Les Garner of Sixus1 Media building most of the main characters) and the storyboard has been approved, the animator sets to work on the sequence of shots required. After trying out a few different camera angles, a quick and dirty test render is done with the Preview renderer set at 256 colors to get a reasonable preview of how the final shot is going to look. Once approved, the individual shots and elements are rendered as QuickTime files with alpha channels and composited in After Effects with the rest of the shot's elements. Characters are not often rendered within a full set; this allows for more control over separate elements for later tweaking.

Step-by-Step Tutorial: Compositing "Rhea" with Adobe After Effects

Poser can, of course, import images and movie footage as background elements, but getting a bit more control over the final shot requires taking the rendered footage into a compositing application. Here, I take a basic look at producing footage in Poser and adding background footage or elements. In this case, I am using Adobe's venerable After Effects. I'm really only skimming the After Effects workflow here due to lack of space, so take a few minutes to read the manual or, better still, get hold of Angie Taylor's excellent book *Creative After Effects 7: Workflow Techniques for Animation, Visual Effects, and Motion Graphics* from Focal Press. It's written for beginners and pros alike.

Anyone familiar with Photoshop will recognize many of After Effects' interface options. The two applications share similar Layer Order and Layer Style options, for example. And, like Poser, both programs use keyframes as the basis for actual animation. Don't be afraid—it's a lot easier than it looks!

1. First, I make a cup of tea. It helps me concentrate. Next, I fire up Poser. In Figure 9.1, I've brought up Rhea, one of the characters from *Dominator X* (see my chapter on the included DVD for selected scenes), but this procedure will work with any character or prop.

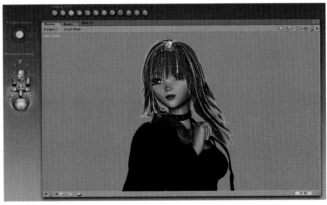

Figure 9.1 The *Dominator X* character Rhea in high-definition format.

TIP

Here, I'm in high-definition (HD) format (hence the wide frame and large screen), but you can set the output ratio and picture size to anything you want. Poser can output animation from tiny Web graphics sequences up to 4K film resolution.

2. In Figure 9.2, I check over the materials options in the Material room. I select a "toon" look from the Material room options to give Rhea a more anime-style appearance. There are various options available with the Toon shader. Play around with the settings until you get a style you like, or just stick with the basics for now.

NOTE

You can apply a toon look to the entire character with just a couple of clicks. First, select the character/prop with the Eyedropper. Next, click on the Set Up Toon Render wacro while holding down the Shift key. This eliminates having to individually select every material, which is a great timesaver!

3. In Figure 9.3, I'm back in the Pose room. I'm positioning the character's actions over the duration of the shot; here, I have Rhea tilting her head and smiling over 100 frames. (The Poser manual provides the basic information on setting up animations with the Timeline.) I think that the toon look tends to look best with one white light pointing directly at the character, offset by a few degrees, but, again, this is my own choice!

4. In Figure 9.4, I choose my Rendering options. It's important to select Black in the Render Over drop-down menu. You'll see why in the next stage. I also select the Remove backfacing polys option to speed up rendering time.

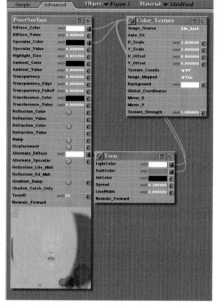

Figure 9.2 Select a toon look in the Material room.

Figure 9.3 Animate the character's actions and light the figure.

TONY LUKE

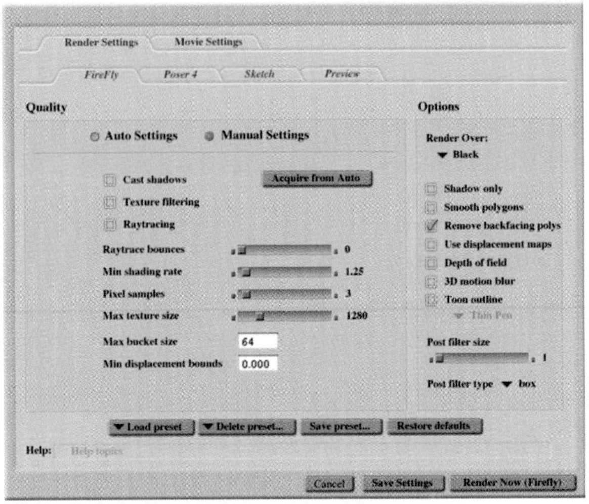

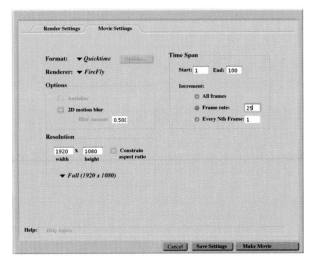

Figure 9.4 Render the figure.

Figure 9.5 Make Movie render settings.

5. In Figure 9.5, I select Make Movie from the Animation menu, and up pops the movie rendering options. I always select the FireFly render engine if I'm using the toon style from the Material room. I add a little motion blur and then type the numerical values for the required output size. (Here again, I've typed in high-definition settings, but 720×576 is fine for most standard-definition projects.) In the Time Span panel, I check that the Start and End frames are to my satisfaction. I'm after the Frame Rate; it can be as fast or slow as I like. I work in PAL format, so I've typed 25 frames per second. (NTSC is 29.97 frames per second.) I click the Make Movie button.

6. Up pops the QuickTime options window. Figure 9.6 is where I tell my computer what it's going to be working on for the next few hours/minutes/days.

I select Animation in the Compression Type drop-down menu. Then I check that Frames per Second is still the same as my choice in the previous window. Next, in the Compressor section, I select the Millions of Colors+ option and Best Quality. The + adds an alpha channel to the shot, which makes my life nice and easy when taking the finished, rendered animation into After Effects. I click OK and, depending on the size, length, and complexity of my shot, I make another cup of tea. Americans should go make some coffee or go to Starbucks at this point.

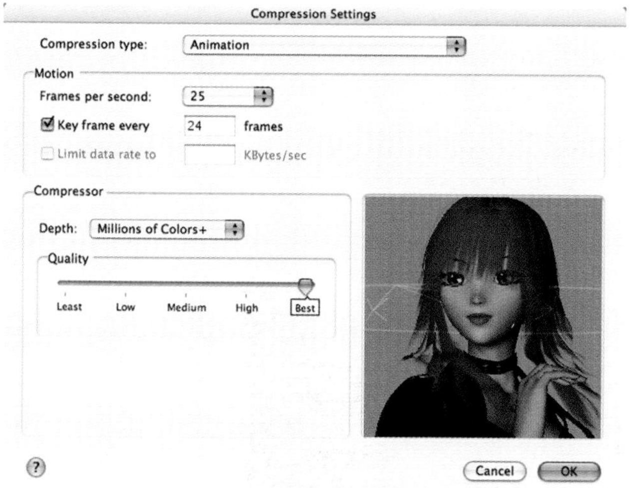

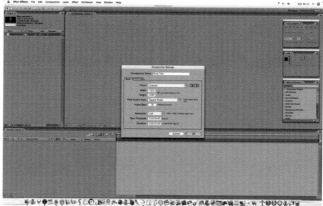

Figure 9.7 Import the Poser movie file into After Effects.

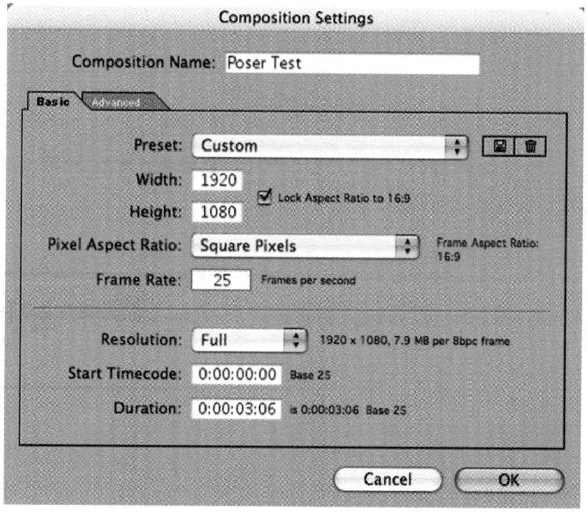

Figure 9.6 QuickTime render compression settings.

1. I now have a rendered movie file sitting on my hard drive. I fire up After Effects. In Figure 9.7, I import the Poser movie into After Effects. The Project window displays a thumbnail of the movie on the top left of the workspace, and it also shows the time, length, and format of the shot. It reads as Millions of Colors +, indicating that the footage has an alpha channel. Next, I select New Composition from the top Composition menu.

2. In Figure 9.8, I type the required values into the Composition Settings window that pops up, making sure that the image dimensions correspond to the size I selected in the movie options in Poser.

Figure 9.8 Match the Composition Settings values.

TONY LUKE

3. In Figure 9.9, I import a piece of background footage for Rhea to stand against. This can be movie footage or a still image. It appears in the Project window. Next, I drag the Rhea footage to the Timeline on the lower half of After Effects' workspace. This is where I find similarities with Photoshop, as the footage effectively becomes a layer. I also drag the background footage to the Timeline and make sure it's sitting below the (Rhea) shot I rendered earlier. The Poser character is now sitting on top of the background, and the black background has vanished. This is because I rendered the Poser footage with the + option earlier on to give it an alpha channel and avoid tedious keying.

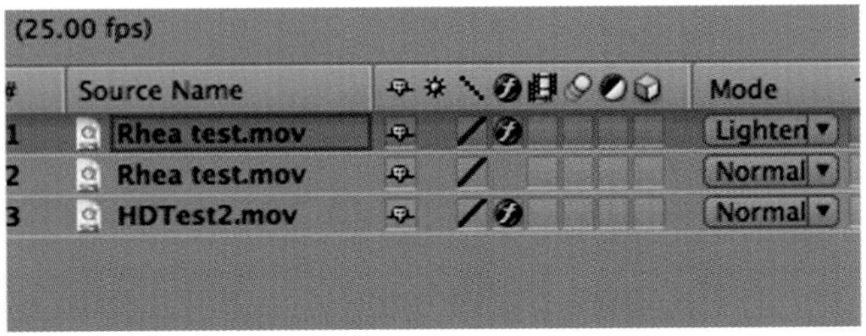

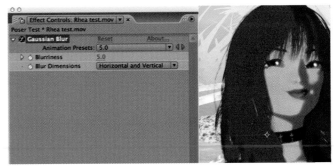

Figure 9.10 Duplicate the Poser layer and set the mode of the upper one to Lighten.

Figure 9.9 Import the background movie footage or still image.

4. At this point, I could skip the next couple of steps and go straight to the final output phase, but these steps show how I achieve a smoother look in the final shot. In the Timeline, I select the Poser footage and duplicate it from the Edit drop-down menu. I now have two identical layers sitting on top of a separate background layer. Then I change the upper Poser layer to Lighten using the Mode tab's drop-down options. See Figure 9.10.

5. From the Effects drop-down menu at the top of the screen, I select Gaussian Blur from the Blur options (very similar to Photoshop!) and move the slider by 5 pixels or so. See Figure 9.11.

Figure 9.11 Gaussian blur by 5 pixels.

6. The character's face now appears a bit hazy. Returning to the Timeline, I click on the upper layer's options arrow, and various values appear. I select Opacity and adjust to taste. 50 percent seems to be a nice all-rounder. I've just "bloomed" the footage! See Figure 9.12.

NOTE

Blooming is the technique of overlaying a duplicate of the original layer on top of itself, setting that new "top" layer to Lighten or Screen, and popping a bit of Gaussian blur on it. You get a nice ethereal look that has the added advantage of smoothing out any "jaggies" that the original image may have. It works just as well in Photoshop as it does for animation files in After Effects.

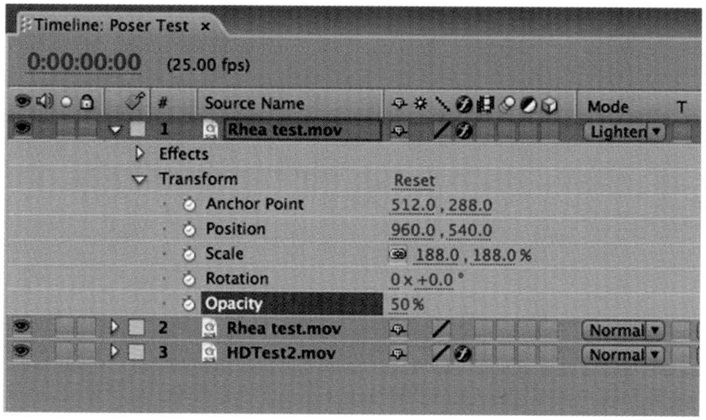

Figure 9.13 Preview and Make Movie.

Figure 9.12 Reduce the upper layer's opacity to 50%.

TIP

Take the plunge with After Effects. It's an incredibly versatile application, and I've really only scratched the surface of its abilities here. The budding Miyazakis out there should also check out Apple's Motion program. The same techniques described here also apply there. Have fun!

7. I usually play around with the footage to my heart's content, adding effects and motion via keyframes. In Figure 9.13, I'm finally happy with the shot. I can either select Preview or go straight to Make Movie (both in the Composition drop-down menu, at the top of the screen). I click Render, and that's it! Figure 9.14 is the final image.

MOTION GRAPHICS

Figure 9.14 Rhea character from *Dominator X* final image.

Insights

Lighting

Unless the scene demands otherwise, I tend to use a single-point light source for most of my shots. I just like what can be achieved with something simple. And with the Toon shader, it's a useful setup. It's possible to achieve very "manga-esque" tones on figures with just one light. For best results, I tend to set Intensity at 110 percent and Map Size at 1024 pixels, with the Shadow on Depth Map at 12.0. This gives a good base image. When put through After Effects with a little "blooming," the results can be very nice indeed.

Content

Being a diehard manga and anime fan, I was delighted when the original Anime Posette went on sale. It was the first off-the-shelf Poser character that I felt truly comfortable working with. I used it as the basis for a number of characters in the first *Dominator* movie back in 2001. Since then, I've been blessed with Aiko and Hiro, which have made the creation of original manga-styled art that much easier. Thanks, DAZ.

My favorite online shop (apart from Content Paradise) would have to be Sixus1 Media (Les Garner). There's not a more crazy and wonderful selection of monsters and beasties available for use in Poser anywhere else on the Web. Les imbues his creations with a degree of dark humor, which is why Renga Media hired him to do the character models on our upcoming feature film *Dominator X*.

Backups

Everything that I produce seems to involve a totally different set of parameters, but I save vast amounts of time by keeping a regular backup of the Runtime folder on a separate hard drive, just in case our main machine dies on us, taking all our precious work and assets with it to Computer Hell. Backups are so important. And as regular purchasers of online material, we always keep the original product installer safe somewhere. As a rule, if it's mechanical, then at some point It Will Go Wrong, and you'll need backups.

Q&A

What advice do you have for artists starting out with Poser?

Poser is something of a rule-breaker. Until recently, it's been seen by some as a toy application. Those in the know, however, have always been aware of its capabilities. It all depends on what you're trying to achieve. The important thing for first-timers to remember is that if it feels right to you, it probably is. Break the rules, and remember to have fun. Poser can be as simple or as complicated as you like. Newcomers are always surprised how little time it takes to get a figure moving about on the screen. I know I was.

Where do you think computer-generated imagery will be 5–10 years from now?

Regular CGI will go from strength to strength until the differences between what's real and imagined will be nonexistent. I have high hopes for Jim Cameron's explorations into 3D.

It would be damn cool to have a 3D system that didn't fry the viewers' eyeballs. Right now, though, I think we'll see a retreat from the standard CGI "look" that's crept in these past couple of years. How many movies released recently look like they came from the same render farm? Too many. I have high hopes that movies like the excellent French animated movie *Renaissance* and the upcoming *Appleseed* sequel will continue to push the boundaries of what's possible in more stylized productions.

Resources

On the DVD

- Artist Gallery
- Video clip: Scenes from *Dominator X* animation

Links

- http://www.aintitcool.com/
- http://www.heavymetal.com/
- http://www.sixus1media.com/
- http://www.renderosity.com
- http://www.mypetskeleton.com/

TONY LUKE

Studio

Software: Poser, Cinema 4D, Shade, Vue Infinite, particleIllusion, After Effects, Motion, Bryce, Photoshop

Hardware: Numerous PowerMac G5s, Xserve RAID, Kona HD output card (for viewing high-definition footage), RenderFarm.net, etc. etc., plus copious amounts of tea

Contact

Tony Luke ■ Renga Media ■ Brighton, East Sussex, England ■ info@rengamedia.com ■ http://www.rengamedia.com

TONY LUKE

MOTION GRAPHICS

Gallery

"Dominator."

"Ghost."

MOTION GRAPHICS

"Dominator."

"Dominator."

MOTION GRAPHICS

"Dominator."

"Extricator & Decimator."

MOTION GRAPHICS

"Dominator."

"Dominator."

MOTION GRAPHICS

"Dominator."

"Dominator."

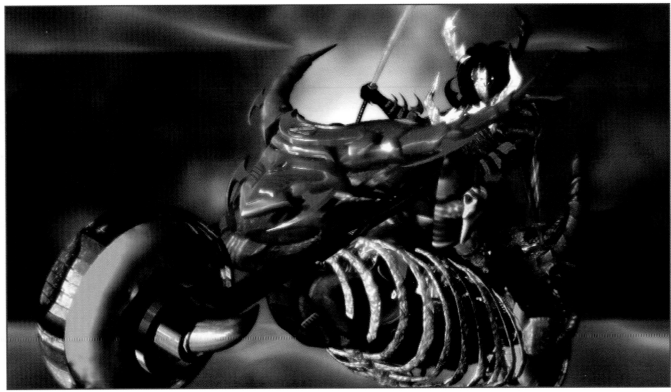

"Hell Hog."

"Girlies."

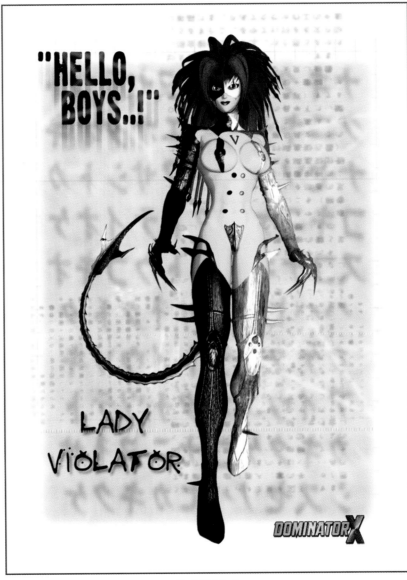

"Lady Violater."

"Vyridia."

MOTION GRAPHICS

"Girls."

"Geisha."

©2006 · GABRIEL SABLOFF · ALL RIGHTS RESERVED

GABRIEL SABLOFF

About the Artist

Gabriel Sabloff is an award-winning filmmaker and illustrator currently based in Los Angeles. He was born and raised in New England and earned his degree in film production from Ithaca College in upstate New York.

Gabriel moved to Los Angeles after college and soon became one of the foremost designers of live hip-hop concerts. His clients include 50 Cent, Jay-Z, Missy Elliott, Mary J. Blige, Nelly, Nas, Diddy, and many more.

He is a founding member of Untamed Cinema, an independent film production company. He co-produced and was director of photography on the extremely popular short film, *Grayson* (2004).

Gabriel has currently begun a new venture, channeling all his talents and experience into Tirade Studios, a new company dedicated to producing spectacular 3D animated feature films.

Artist's Statement

My approach to all my artistic endeavors is extremely simple minded. I just ask myself, "Does it look cool yet?" If the answer is no, I'll keep working on whatever it is until it excites me. Then I have to trust that what excites me will excite my audience.

I can't help but roll my eyes at discussions of art theory, academia, and psychology. Art is not that complicated and should not be overanalyzed. It's not surprising then that I have always drifted toward the realm of fantasy art. As a genre, it celebrates only two things: talent and imagination—two aspects that are conspicuously absent in the majority of modern art.

Influences

I could cite some worldly, noble goal about why I create art and film, but that would be pretentious. I create art because it makes me happy. It is a blessing to be able to receive acceptance, admiration, and employment doing something that comes easily. As for my influences, all artists are the sum of a lifetime of experiences and influences. I don't think it would be fair to drop just a few names.

"Portrait of Villainy."

Techniques

The Creative Process

My creative process is probably the same as most artists: a lot of brainstorming, panic, cursing, vast consumption of caffeine, soul searching, wild inspiration, giddiness, disappointment, denial, more panic and cursing, a burst of insight, and finally acceptance.

In terms of my workflow, Poser is the production stage of my films. Everything before Poser is preproduction on paper and Photoshop; everything after Poser is postproduction in Final Cut Pro and After Effects.

Step-by-Step Tutorial: 3D Cinematography "Portrait of Villainy"

By comparison to many 3D artists and filmmakers, I am pretty untechnical. I just want to be a kid playing in a sandbox with his action figures. Poser is the perfect tool for someone like me who is from a live-action film and illustration background but has no formal training in the 3D arts.

Just as the art of modeling and rigging is a mystery to me, many 3D artists find the art of cinematography a challenge they are unprepared for. This is unfortunate because it's possible to be the most skilled 3D artist or animator in the world, but without knowing how to photograph the work effectively, it will never reach its full potential.

I created the final image shown in Figure 10.25 as a teaser poster for my new feature film that is being created and rendered completely with Poser. I designed this character on paper and then hired two 3D artists to create it. Daniel Bacchiocchi did the modeling, and Keith Young did the rigging, UV mapping, and all-around troubleshooting.

While the creation of the character was a technical odyssey that I barely understand, the result is an "action figure" for my sandbox. Now it is up to me to bring him to life onscreen.

I invite you to go step by step through this image with me. Along the way, I'll try to demystify the basics of cinematography.

1. In Figure 10.1, I import the figure, his dynamic coat, and sword. I set up the coat and sword earlier as *smart props*.

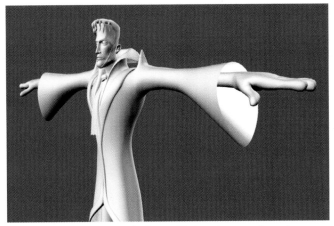

Figure 10.1 Import the figure with dynamic coat and sword.

> **TIP**
>
> *Smart props* are objects that "remember" the figure they were attached to and the way they were attached to that figure.

2. In Figure 10.2, I pose my figure into a cool, super-villain pose. I hide the coat while I am posing to make it easier to select his body parts. Bending my figure's legs properly requires a variable of –50 bend on the thigh and 50 bend on the shin.

NOTE

If you have IK chains turned on and the legs are bending oddly, it is probably due to poor figure setup. One way to correct this is to lower the Y axis of the hip until the legs are at their most out-of-whack. Then select the thigh and the shin body parts in turn and slowly finesse the Bend parameter dials of both until the leg appears to be bending properly.

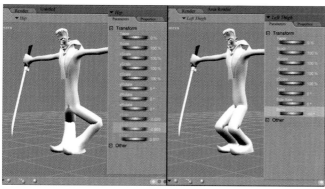

Figure 10.2 Bend the legs after lowering the Y axis of the hips.

TIP

Always use the parameter dials when moving and posing your figure so that you can stay in control and only affect one variable at a time. Using the visual interface to grab and move your figure can become confusing and create movement that you did not intend.

You can use the up and down arrow keys to toggle through a character's body parts while posing.

3. In Figure 10.3, I import the background set and position my super-villain by the arched doorway. For this scene, I am using DAZ 3D's Courtyard set.

Figure 10.3 Import the background set and position the figure.

Cinematography Lesson 1: Composition

Imagine if every major element in your frame were flattened into a featureless paper cutout. Figures, sets, sky, highlights, shadows, colors, everything—all flattened into light and dark shapes. Would your picture still be interesting to look at in this state? Take away the subject matter, the action, the hot girls, the slick rendering, the bump-mapping, the reflections, and other effects, and you are left with composition. I'm not going to try to explain *how* to make a good composition here. People who are a lot smarter than me have written volumes on that subject. All I can say is expose yourself to a lot of great artist's work and learn from them.

MOTION GRAPHICS

4. Next, I run a quick cloth simulation to get the coat swinging and choose a frame where the coat is in an interesting position.

TIP

In my experience with cloth sims, the combination of stretch damping and cloth density is the most crucial. Cloth density controls the "heaviness" of the cloth, while stretch damping defines how much the cloth can stretch. If the density is high and the stretch damping low, the cloth will sag and bounce like it is made of rubber. If the density is low and stretch damping high, the cloth will barely move, as if it were made of paper.

5. I set the document window size to an appropriate aspect ratio for my portrait.

6. With the frame sized correctly, I now select the dolly camera. Since this is a still frame, the first thing I do is turn off camera animation. Then, using the camera interface controls, I move the camera into roughly the desired position. I finesse the camera into its final composition using the parameter dials: Trans X, Y, Z, Roll, Pitch, Yaw, and Focal. See Figure 10.4

TIP

The dolly camera is the best camera to use for 90 percent of all your photographs and animations. The pan and tilt controls move the way a real camera dolly would move.

Figure 10.4 Move the dolly camera to the desired position.

Cinematography Lesson 2: Focal Length

Focal length is one of the most important tools of the photographer. Use it wisely. In Poser, this control is the Focal parameter dial. Poser's cameras are set up to emulate a real camera lens, so all the same rules of photography apply in the 3D realm. Here are the general rules.

The midpoint focal length of most camera lenses is 50mm (Focal 50). The concept of a 50mm lens is that when you look through it, it is like looking through a window. There should be no magnification or distortion of the image. It should emulate the way the human eye sees the world.

Anything above a 50mm lens is considered a telephoto lens—objects far away become magnified. See Figure 10.5. This magnification also causes another phenomenon: The planes of the foreground and background seem to compress, creating a feeling of flatness. This effect is flattering on a human face; therefore, most portraits are shot with telephoto lenses. Telephoto lenses can create some of the most gorgeous pictures, but they are the most under-used in 3D art. For most people, it seems logical to move the camera closer for a close-up. In fact, you should do the opposite. For close-ups, you should move the camera as far back as possible and zoom in using the Focal dial.

Figure 10.5 Telephoto is any focal length above 50mm.

Any lens less than 50mm is considered a wide-angle lens. Wide angles do the opposite of Telephoto lenses: They expand the distance between foreground and background objects. See Figure 10.6. They also create a radial distortion at the edges of the frame. Extreme wide angles result in crazy fish-eye views. While wide angles are not desired for beauty shots, they can be spectacular in an action scene. The distortion of the wide-angle lens is also well suited for comedy.

Figure 10.6 Wide angle is any focal length less than 50mm.

MOTION GRAPHICS

Now that the figure is posed in front of the background just right, the dynamic coat is frozen in a cool position, and the camera is set, I begin to think about my lighting scheme. I want this to be a shadowy night scene, so I decide to go with several small spotlights to ensure plenty of dark areas in between.

TIP

Once you have things set just right, you might want to use the Lock Actor option to lock off body parts, cameras, or lights to avoid moving items by accident.

7. In Figure 10.7, I delete all existing lights to start with a completely dark stage. Then I create a new light. This is my "key" light. It does the most to define the main object of interest in the scene. I place this light off to one side and above the figure to ensure that half of the figure's face is cast in deep shadows. I set this light to 125 percent intensity to slightly overexpose my textures and make the figure really pop out of the darkness. See Figure 10.8.

TIP

Remember to use the Selection Render tool. You will save a lot of time by rendering just that small piece of the scene you are working on.

Figure 10.7 Turn off all lights except one; this is your key light.

Figure 10.8 The key light is set at 125 percent intensity to slightly overexpose.

8. Having a clear separation between foreground and back-ground is important in professional photography. In most cases, the subject shouldn't blend into the background. In Figure 10.9, I add a second light behind and to the left of the figure (pointing back toward the camera).

Figure 10.9 Add a second light, a rim light, pointing back toward the camera.

TIP

To properly control and analyze what each light is doing, it is smart to turn off all the previous lights while you are placing a new one. You can quickly turn a light on or off by clicking on the light's position circle while holding down the Alt key.

This second light is called a rim light because it creates a strip of light around the edge of your figure. For dramatic effect, I have made this a "hot" light and cranked up its intensity to 200 percent. See Figure 10.10 for the effect.

Figure 10.10 Set the rim light's intensity to 200 percent.

TIP

The brightness slider on the light controls only goes up to 100 percent. At 100 percent, your textures appear at their "normal" brightness—the same that they would look if you opened them in a paint program. To increase a light's brightness past 100 percent, open the light's parameter dials and use the "intensity" dial.

GABRIEL SABLOFF

9. In Figure 10.11, I illuminate the background. I want to keep things dark and shadowy, so I create a third spotlight, a background light, and position it to point down at the arch at about a 45-degree angle.

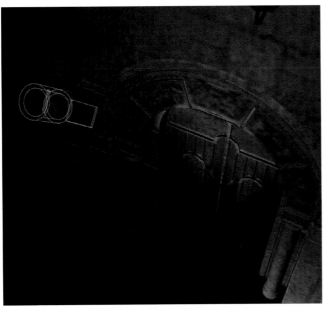

Figure 10.11 Add a spotlight to illuminate the background

In Figure 10.12, I color the light blue and play with the "angle end" and "distance end" until the light covers as much of the arch as I want.

Figure 10.12 Color and adjust the background light.

10. The lighting is looking pretty cool now, but the shape of my villain's head and neck-ruff are still getting lost in the shadow of the door behind. To create the proper separation between foreground and background, I create a fourth spotlight, a detail light, and shine a narrow beam on the door behind the villain's head. See Figure 10.13.

Figure 10.13 Shine a narrow beam on the door behind the villain's head.

I make this light yellow to add some warm contrast to the frosty blues and purples that dominate the scene. See Figure 10.14.

NOTE

All the lights in this scene are set to use raytraced shadows with a Shadow Blur Radius of 2 and a Shadow Min Bias of .2.

Figure 10.14 Color and add contrast.

Now that the lighting is done, in Figure 10.15, it is clear that my villain's eyes are lost in the shadows. I have to remedy this problem and have the character engage the viewer. The eyes are the windows to the soul.

Figure 10.15 The eyes are lost in the dark.

Switch all the eye image maps to the ambient channel.

Figure 10.16 Switch all the eye image maps to the ambient channel.

11. In Figure 10.16, I enter the Material room and switch all the eye image maps from the diffuse channel to the ambient channel.

The ambient channel makes the texture self-illuminating. So, at an ambient value of 1, the texture appears at its "normal" brightness, independent of any lights in the scene. It's the perfect effect for a comic book villain. See Figure 10.17.

TIP

Keep your main diffuse color connected to the image map, even if your Diffuse value is zero. Disconnecting the main diffuse from the image map causes the texture to appear blank in the preview window.

Figure 10.17 Bring the villain to life!

Figure 10.18 The lighting looks a little too typical.

It is all looking fine now, but the look of the lighting is too typical. See Figure 10.18. I'm not aiming for realism here. I want a "harder," more unique, comic book-style for my villain. So I use one of my secret techniques.

12. I add a Toon shader node to the Alternate Diffuse channel and set Spread to .04 to give the shadows a nice, hard edge. But instead of turning off the main diffuse, I turn it down to .5, thereby maintaining a hint of the subtleties in the model that would be lost if I went with a pure toon-shaded look. I also connect both the Diffuse Color and the Toon shader to the Image Map node, resulting in a unique, comic book look. See Figure 10.19 for the settings. The power of Poser lies in experiments like this. I found this combination by days of trial and error on a previous project. I encourage you to invent your own techniques. See Figure 10.20 for the result.

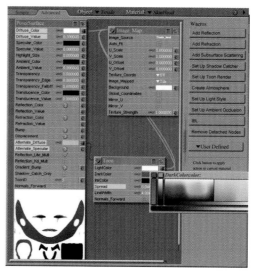

Figure 10.19 Add a Toon shader node to the Alternate Diffuse channel.

NOTE

The Set Up Toon Render wacro changes texture settings and render settings that you may not find desirable. I recommend adding the Toon shader node manually.

NOTE

A *wacro* is a custom PoserPython script used within the Shader window to create new material types.

13. I am pretty much happy with everything, but I find the ground texture boring, so I add a reflection to the ground texture. I simply click the default Add Reflection wacro, and then I set Reflection Value to .5 and BG Color to a dull purple. See Figure 10.21 for the settings and Figure 10.22 for the result.

Figure 10.20 A unique look, created.

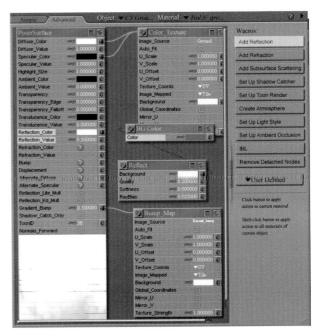

Figure 10.21 Add Reflection wacro settings.

Figure 10.22 The modified ground texture.

14. I'm almost done, but I feel the image still could use that special something to make it unique. So I use another one of my secret techniques and render two sketch renders that I set up earlier. Figures 10.23 and 10.24 show the sketch renders.

Figure 10.23 Sketch render one.

TIP

When using reflections, remember to add at least one raytrace bounce to your render settings, or no reflection will occur.

15. In Photoshop, I blend these sketch renders with the main render, blend in a grunge map or two, adjust the levels, and voilà! Figure 10.25 shows my final image.

Figure 10.24 Sketch render two.

©2006 · GABRIEL SABLOFF · ALL RIGHTS RESERVED

Figure 10.25 "Portrait of Villainy" final poster image.

Insights

Lighting

The scene in this technique did not call for it, but a fill light is one of the most commonly used lights. It "fills in" the shadows so they do not appear pitch black. Pure black shadows are not usually desirable except in a film noir scene like this one.

Exposure

Poser's cameras do have an f-stop parameter dial, but I do not recommend using it, as the brightening and darkening effect does not appear in the preview window. Instead, change the intensity of the lights to change the brightness of the image. Exposure also affects depth of field, which I'll talk about later.

A properly exposed image should have a wide range of lights and darks, from the absolute brightest highlights (the maximum white your monitor can produce) to the absolute deepest shadows (the maximum black your monitor can produce). Use these extremes sparingly, because all detail is lost in these zones. Most colors and tones should fall somewhere between the whitest white and the blackest black.

Images that have no bright areas or highlights are called *underexposed*, while images that possess no deep shadows are called *overexposed*. Neither case is desirable. Always shoot for a full range of tones.

Also, be wary of super-saturating colors. If a color is too intense, it can wreak havoc when printing or exporting a movie. What looks good on a computer monitor may not look good on a printout or a TV monitor.

Depth of Field

Depth of field refers to the relationship between the focus of objects in a scene. By default, everything is in focus to the 3D camera. This is called a *deep focus*. The opposite is called *shallow*

focus. Shallow focus means that there is only a small slice of the scene in focus, while the rest is blurry. This effect is common in film but is much rarer in 3D photography due to the complexity and computing power needed to simulate the effect.

I recommend against trying to achieve depth of field in a 3D render. If possible, it's better to render the foreground and background elements in separate passes and composite them together in another application where blurriness can be applied.

Content

I don't use the stock Poser content that much. The figures and their textures are excellent and are great for running quick tests. But stylistically, I prefer things to be darker and edgier. I am a huge fan of all the user-made content available on the Web. It would cost ten of thousands of dollars to have a dozen sets and props built from scratch. With the online content available to Poser artists, it's possible to buy everything needed for just a few hundred dollars. I shop at all the regular spots, including DAZ 3D, Renderosity, Content Paradise, 3D Cafe, and Turbo Squid.

The Cloth Room

The simulation settings are a daunting challenge but just require patience. Spending the hours or days needed to get a cloth looking right is well worth it. When a character has dynamic clothing, I create a benchmark animation that puts the cloth sim through every eventuality—slow movements, quick movements, spinning movements, extreme stretching and compression, changes in inertia and velocity to the entire figure, and so on. I call this my "stress test." The goal is to find the right cloth sim settings to survive the entire sequence without tearing, crashing, bunching up, or freaking out in general. I also recommend creating hair out of cloth simulations. The hair system is fine for still images, but for animation, the hair simulation is flawed in several significant ways.

GABRIEL SABLOFF

Q&A

What advice do you have for artists who are starting out with Poser?

Don't listen to snooty friends who say that only a higher-end 3D application can output great 3D art. Poser is a powerful tool in the right hands. Using smart props, material groups, and the Area Render tool are three ways to really save time. Take time to learn the program inside and out, and it will be very rewarding.

What do you wish someone had told you when you first started with Poser?

1. Always save before starting a render or dynamic simulation.

2. I wish someone had told me about the Lock Actor switch as well as the Memorize and Restore functions.

3. It's easy to overlook the "silhouette" display style. But it's a great tool for exporting a rotoscoping matte to use in After Effects.

4. In the Collide Against window of the Cloth room, it took me a long time to figure out that the parameter dials there are not global settings. They are specific to the currently selected collision object. Duh.

Where do you think computer-generated imagery will be 5–10 years from now?

I sure hope it will be in 360-degree virtual environments. C'mon, tech monkeys. The technology is here. I want to see some spectacular VR before I go. VR is still being ignored by all the big developers since it failed to launch in the 90s. I think when it finally hits, it will change everything about how we view art and media for the next few hundred years.

What is one of the biggest challenges you have faced while using Poser, and how do you solve the issue?

The parameter dials in the Cloth and Hair rooms have no visual or intuitive methodology. Some of the dials effect a dramatic change over a few hundredths degrees, while others require a few hundred degrees for a noticeable change. The only way to solve these puzzles is to do meticulous charting of a dynamic behavior over the course of many test simulations.

What are the hardest postures, gestures, and expressions to create and why? Describe your process in posing your figures.

The hardest poses are those that require extreme stretching of the body or hyperextensions. Most figures are not rigged to perform well at the extreme limits of human body movement. That's a shame because as any artist who deals with comic books, action, or fantasy will tell you, you almost always want to exaggerate the motions of your character for dramatic effect.

In posing figures, I always start with the hip. The hip determines the figure's weight distribution, direction, and elevation. Then I move to the feet and position them to complement the hip position. After that, I roughly pose the abdomen, chest, and shoulders. The chest and shoulders are especially important in establishing the counterbalance to what the hip is doing. I pay special attention to the shoulders, as they are instrumental in establishing the figure's attitude: happy, sad, proud, angry, scared, shy, and so on. All these emotions can be emulated with the position of the shoulders.

After the shoulders, I move on to the arms and forearms, neck, and head. After that, I usually wait to see what the final camera position is before articulating the face and hands. There's no need to do all that work if the camera's not going to see it.

Resources

On the DVD

- Music Video: "Lil Jon: Crunkwar"
- Animation clip: "Double Take"
- Animation clip: Cloth Simulation Stress Test

Links

- http://www.conceptart.org
- http://www.deviantart.com

GABRIEL SABLOFF

Studio

Software: Poser, Photoshop, Final Cut Pro, After Effects

Hardware: PC, Mac G4

Contact

Gabriel Sabloff ■ Redmonkey Pictures, Untamed Cinema, Tirade Studios ■ Glendale, CA ■ gabe@untamedcinema.com ■ www.redmonkeypictures.com ■ www.untamedcinema.com

Modeler

Daniel Bacchiocchi ■ dbacs2194@msn.com

MOTION GRAPHICS

Gallery

"Crunkwar" still.

"Crunkwar" still.

MOTION GRAPHICS

"Crunkwar" still.

"Crunkwar" still.

MOTION GRAPHICS

"Crunkwar" still.

"Crunkwar" still.

MOTION GRAPHICS

"Crunkwar" still.

"Grid Iron" still.

MOTION GRAPHICS

"Grid Iron" still.

"Grid Iron" still.

"Grid Iron" still.

"Showdown Chasm" still.

MOTION GRAPHICS

"Ways of the Wicked" still.

"Ways of the Wicked" still.

"Ways of the Wicked" still.

"Ways of the Wicked" still.

"Ways of the Wicked" still.

"Ways of the Wicked" still.

"Ways of the Wicked" still.

JOHN TAYLOR DISMUKES

About the Artist

John Taylor Dismukes has earned three degrees: fine art print making from Mesa College, fine art painting from San Diego State University, and illustration from the prestigious Art Center College of Design, where he graduated with distinction and honors. John has combined his fine art and illustration focuses and created a unique style, enabling him to launch several smash-hit, one-man shows and create a successful business enterprise. He also has two cutting edge T-shirt lines and a jewelry line that reflects his signature "gothic tech" look.

John has been president of Capstone Studios, Inc., for the past 20 years. He and his partner, Jo-Anne Redwood, have made Capstone one of the top national design studios. Capstone is well recognized in the entertainment and hospitality industries, winning numerous awards for print, motion graphics, and concept design.

Over the span of John's career, the awards are too numerous to list, but highlights include Belding, Key Art Awards, Corporate Identity, LULU, and Grammy Awards to name a few. Most recently, John's painting "Ozzy Osbourne: Prince of Darkness" was part of an exhibit The Greatest Album Covers That Never Were that toured the world for two years, ending up in the Rock 'n Roll Hall of Fame.

Artist's Statement

My approach to art is the same as my approach to life: Take No Prisoners. I am an art junkie. I study the past, but I'm also always looking for the new-edge designs. My style has been termed "gothic tech" and is basically mixing old with new. I've studied the works of Caravaggio to Robert Williams and then brought in my own vision to the canvas.

Influences

My motivations stem from trying to capture what's inside my head and bring it into the physical world. My inspirations are many, but to name a few, they would be Caravaggio, Michelangelo, Mucha, Geiger, Jackson Pollack, Robert Rauschenberg, and hot rod designer Big Daddy Roth. When I was a kid, I was influenced by motorcycle gangs (Hells Angels) and low riders. Music was and still is a huge inspiration for me. I spent time at Tower Records just looking at album covers. A huge influence was Frank Frazetta. His Viking imagery inspired me to change from pursuing fine arts to what I'm now known for.

"Viking Good Warlord."

Techniques

The Creative Process

Research, research, research. I take on a project, research every bit of information out there, and then create what hasn't been done. When creating, it's important to take demographics into consideration. If I'm creating a motorcycle, I sit on one, and I talk to people about what they like about them. If I'm creating a game, I play it and talk to the experts about it. I take a lot of notes and photographs and then sit down with a sketchpad, music, sketches, and story of the character I've created and tighten up the sketch. I develop a story about the character and build on that.

Step-by-Step Tutorial: Viking Woman Box Design

My technique mixes photos with 2D and 3D, which makes my images more realistic and prevents them from looking like cliché 3D. I always start my work with sketches to develop the concept and layout and then decide what the best approach is to finish.

1. When I begin a project, I listen to the client's ideas to get an understanding of the project and to conceptualize the artwork. See Figure 11.1.

Figure 11.1 Conceptualize the artwork.

2. This job is for a box design, so I start out by looking at other boxes and consider some beginning concepts. I begin by making some preliminary sketches and getting a direction staked out. My first sketches for this project include a Viking-type woman holding a sword. See Figure 11.2.

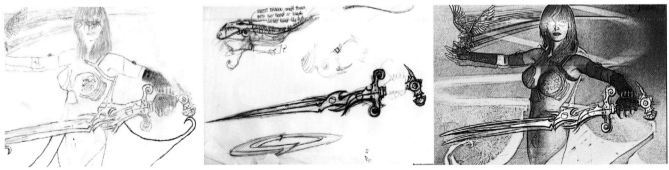

Figure 11.2 Make some preliminary sketches.

3. Now I am ready for Poser. I bring the sketch into Poser as the background of my scene so that I can work on top of the sketch. First, I use a wireframe figure to pose the figure and to make sure the lighting and camera angles are correct for the piece. Then, using a nude figure, I build the image.

> **NOTE**
>
> The projects at Capstone Studios are usually a team effort. Some of the artists in the studio are specialists in certain software, such as Electric Image or 3ds Max, and they make the 3D props such as the armor, clothing, and swords.

I compile the materials and work the lighting again. After that, I export the image as a low-res file into Photoshop. I do everything in separate layers in Photoshop. I save all settings in the image and in each layer and make sure everything matches. Once I have all the elements in place, I show the client. In this case, the client requested some changes, such as to use only the top half of the Viking girl and to use thunderbolts and smoke in the image. See Figure 11.3.

4. I need to think about the assets to be included. Capstone Studios has a lot of swords, armor, and backgrounds. I'm in a Viking and heavy metal phase and luckily have a lot of material to use for this project. See Figure 11.4.

Figure 11.4 Re-use stock content when you can.

Figure 11.3 Save each element in a separate layer.

> **NOTE**
>
> Capstone Studios keeps a fairly large library of content that can be used anytime. Whenever we make props or figures for projects, we put them in the library. We probably have more than 300 beautifully detailed images to use, both 2D and 3D.

5. I need to come up with a few color comps for the client to choose from, so I work in Poser with the figure and try a few different ideas, such as the sphere, glowing eyes, different weapons, and the bird. I like dramatic angles, so I experiment until I get the desired look and feel. I share the comps with the client again to get changes and a final okay.

I add a small 2D figure on a horse in the bottom-left corner to give the image depth, compile some of the assets such as the smoke and clouds with the figure, and present the final image to the client. Figure 11.5 is the final image.

JOHN TAYLOR DISMUKES

Figure 11.5 "Viking Good Girl" final image.

Insights

Lighting

Most of my work has severe, dramatic lighting, and the Poser lighting tools allow me to light my work exactly as I would in a photo studio but with even more flexibility. I do a lot of over-exposing and directional lighting.

Q&A

What are some of your favorite Poser features?

My favorite is the wireframe and easy viewing in wireframe mode. The lighting is incredible, the cameras are beautiful, and the Material room is really neat. Poser is an incredible program that allows me to easily visualize my thoughts.

What are some of your timesaving tips when using Poser on a project or artwork?

Create low-resolution models. I use Poser to generate wireframes and then output low resolution, which I sketch over, adding all my props and background and incorporating Poser sketches when I get to my final phase. Once I've proofed everything, I can create a high-resolution final.

What advice do you have for artists who are starting out with Poser?

Use a big machine with lots of RAM and memory. Read books, ask questions, and look at other people's work that you like. Experiment a lot, and be patient.

Where do you think computer-generated imagery will be 5–10 years from now?

It will be in virtual reality (VR). You'll be able to go inside the VR world, and it will be more real than the real world. There will be brain banks that feed into VR.

Resources

On the DVD

- Artist Gallery

Links

- http://www.creativemagazine.com
- http://www.3dcreativemag.com
- http://www.turbosquid.com
- http://www.daz.com
- http://www.3d02.com
- http://www.fantagraphics.com/artist/williams/williams.html
- http://www.3dtotal.com
- http://www.cgsociety.com

JOHN TAYLOR DISMUKES

Studio

Software: Poser, Photoshop CS2, Illustrator, Maya, Electric Image, Cinema 4D

Hardware: Mac Tower G5s, two 30-inch monitors, memory and RAM cranked to the limit, and Epson printers

Contact

John Taylor Dismukes ■ Capstone Studios, Inc. ■ Irvine, CA ■ JTD@dismukes.com ■ http://www.dismukes.com

JOHN TAYLOR DISMUKES

Gallery

"Viking Ork."

"Viking The Assassin."

"Viking Widow Maker."

"Viking Bone Crusher."

ILLUSTRATION

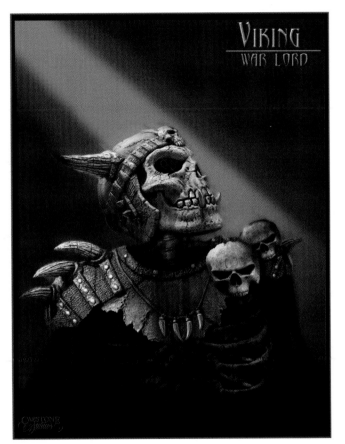

"Viking War Lord."

"Viking Evil Girl."

"Viking Bad Warlord."

"Ozzy Ozbourne: Prince of Darkness" lithograph.

THOMAS WEISS (BETON)

About the Artist

Thomas Weiss (Beton) has more than 40 years of experience with oils, pencils, acrylics, watercolors, airbrush, and now a new medium, computer graphics. His first exhibition of drawings was at the age of 19 in his hometown in Bavaria, Germany. Career highlights include being featured at SIGGRAPH and featured in the first 3D art coffee table book, *Digital Beauties*. Thomas' work has been seen on several book and magazine covers, and his first solo art book is available on his Web page, 3d-fantasy.com. He also founded the art Web site DreamLandWorks.com.

Artist's Statement

I'm a painter. I've painted since I could hold a pencil. I have so many pictures in my head that it is impossible to paint them all in the classical way with oil or pencils. Computer graphics is a great thing. It's faster and easier than painting on canvas. I love art, and I am inspired by humans, so humans are a theme in most of my artwork.

Painting a human character is the best way into the heart of the viewers. Fantasy and portraits are my favorites, and the erotic, too. For me, art is the way to my personal Nirvana, a step closer to paradise. It is my way of telling you my feelings.

Influences

I'm inspired in everything I see, hear, and read. I'm influenced by Georg Weiss, my dad, who is a woodcarver. My favorite artists are Boris Vallejo, Caspar David Friedrich, Chuck Close, Egon Schiele, Steve Hanks, Gustav Klimt, and most of the oriental painters of the nineteenth century.

"Diana."

Techniques

The Creative Process

When I get an idea, I start Poser and create the figure, export the scene as an OBJ file, import the figure into Bryce, and then create the scene around the figure. After that, I search for the best light and camera angle and render the scene. Sometimes it looks completely different from my first idea. After rendering, I do the post work, which is important because I love the soft, painted look. The pure renders are not soft enough for my kind of style.

Step-by-Step Tutorial:
Creating "The Maker" (Fantasy)

1. I create Figure 12.5, "The Maker" image, using Poser, Painter, and Apophysis, which is a freeware fractal flame-generating program. I make a nice fractal render and get the idea to mirror the fractal to make a brain-looking hat. See Figure 12.1.

TIP

You'll learn so much by copying other pictures. Take a closer look at photos and copy the poses. A real-looking pose is much more important than a good texture. Don't use too many different colors in your picture unless it is a scene from a children's birthday party or a circus.

2. I render the alien lady in Poser on a black background. See Figure 12.2.

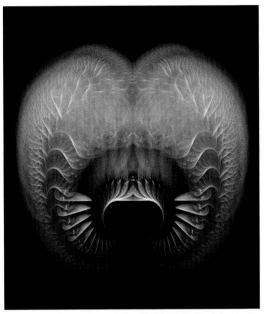

Figure 12.1 Mirror the fractal.

Figure 12.2 Render the alien figure—no hair needed—in Poser.

TIP

Disable shadows and bump maps for test renders.

3. In Figure 12.3, I cut out the fractal hat in Painter and put it on the Poser alien woman's head.

Figure 12.3 Cut the fractal hat in Painter so that it fits on the alien's head.

4. I do a little post work in Painter, such as blurring the edges and correcting the colors.

5. In Figure 12.4, I make a transparency map (trans map) of the whole thing in Painter or Paint Shop Pro. Using the rendered picture, I convert it into a black-and-white picture.

Then I increase the contrast and highlights until I get a two-color picture—one that is completely black and white with no grays. Sometimes I also have to paint over areas with black and white to get the result I want.

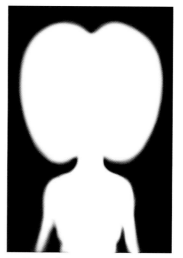

Figure 12.4 Make a transparency map in Painter.

6. I load the picture with the trans map back into Poser and use it as a Texture Map node plugged into the Transparency channel in the Material room.

7. Finally, I select another Apophysis fractal render to use as the background. After rendering the whole scene, I do a little more post work in Painter again. I soften the edges and change the colors a little bit. Figure 12.5 shows the final image of "The Maker."

Figure 12.5 "The Maker" final image.

Figure 12.6 Create the Poser character using a photo as the background.

Step-by-Step Tutorial:
Creating "Jessi in the Garden" (Realism)

1. In Figure 12.8, "Jessi in the Garden," you can see a realistic-looking picture using a photo as the background. First, in Figure 12.6, I create the Poser character on the stairs.

2. In Figure 12.7, I export the scene as an OBJ file, import it into Bryce, and select a 2D plane with the garden photo for the background. I always disable the shadow options for the background planes. That's one of the things I like very much in Bryce. You can change the shadow options for every object.

Figure 12.7 Insert the garden photo as a background in Bryce.

> ## NOTE
>
> Using photos for backgrounds adds realism to simulate the lighting of the photo.

3. For the lighting in this image, I use a lot of soft lights from different directions—the most from behind to simulate a sunny day. I also place some 2D and 3D plants in the foreground and behind the stairs.

4. After rendering the scene, I do post work with Painter again. I soften the edges, correct the colors, and post work the woman's hair with a hair retouching brush. For the hair retouching, I use a ready-made brush in Painter called "smeary round." I also use the "fine air brush" tool pretty often. You can see the final image in Figure 12.8.

Figure 12.8 "Jessi in the Garden" final image.

Insights

Lighting

I usually render in Bryce, but I use a self-made light set in Poser that is composed of 22 different spots from all directories to simulate global lighting. If I render in Poser, it's only for portraits, because the soft shadows are good for these kinds of pictures. Sometimes I use a single spotlight. I always try to create a dramatic light. The pure frontlight is a bit boring.

Content

Without props and other content, you can only make nudes. That's why content is so important. I only work with prebuilt content except for the trees. For the trees, I use the program Xfrog. I use content of Renderosity, DAZ 3D, and Runtime DNA. I like the Victoria 3 character very much. You can save hair as a prop file, which makes it possible to use different hair prop on the same character at once and mix your own hairstyle.

Q&A

Where do you think computer-generated imagery will be 5–10 years from now?

Everything is possible, from the artful painting to the digital copy of a real human in perfect quality. The handling of the programs is getting easier, and the quality is getting much better. Imagination is the only limit. Art has no rules.

What advice do you have for artists who are starting out with Poser?

Don't do too much! Start with easy poses and simple lights. Try to copy other pictures. That's helpful, and you can learn a lot that way. Also, be sure you know what your client wants before you begin working on a project to save time on revisions. I once had to create the same picture more than five times because I didn't know what the client wanted.

What are the hardest postures, gestures, and expressions to create and why?

Creating natural-looking characters is always hard because none of the Poser characters has enough morphs. A little secret is that you can save a hair prop *hr2 as a normal prop *pp2 and use two or three different hairs on the same figure.

Resources

On the DVD

- Artist Gallery

Links

- http://www.renderosity.com
- http://www.3dcommune.com
- http://www.runtimedna.com
- http://www.daz3d.com
- http://www.dreamlandworks.com

THOMAS WEISS (BETON)

Studio

Software: Poser, Bryce, Painter, Paint Shop Pro, Apophysis

Hardware: Wacom Sketchboard, Athlon 3000 64+ with 1GB RAM ATI Radeon 9600 with 256MB

Contact

Thomas Weiss (Beton) ■ Kaufbeuren, Bavaria, Germany ■ moerteltom@t-online.de ■ www.3d-fantasy.com

Gallery

"African Woman."

"Evil Heart."

"Valkyr."

FANTASY, PHOTO-REALISM

"Look What I Found."

"My Doom."

THOMAS WEISS (BETON)

FANTASY, PHOTO-REALISM

"Romantic."

"Toreador."

"Inspiration."

THOMAS WEISS (BETON)

MIKE CAMPAU

About the Artist

At 3 years old, Mike won first place in a local McDonald's drawing contest. That's where it all began! Later on, he received his bachelor's of fine arts with an emphasis in design and digital imaging from the University of Michigan. For the past 10 years, he has served as creative director of SeventhStreet near Detroit in Birmingham, Michigan. Most SeventhStreet clients are involved in the automotive industry. Mike thinks of Poser as a great creative release. Career highlights include taking first place in the 1994 Gannet Outdoor Board Contest and 2003 and 2004 Gold CADDY Awards.

Artist's Statement

I consider myself not only an artist but a technician. I'm always trying to find the best way to make something look real, but typically, it is never the easiest solution. That's why I'm constantly learning, looking, and trying to take the next step. The thing that distinguishes the really good artists from the great artists is the detail that nobody notices but that makes all the difference in the world.

Influences

I love creating art on the computer, and lucky me, I get to do it for a living! For inspiration, I don't have to look any further than my family, Krista, Emma, Nate, and Ansley.

"Unleash Your Horses" Quaker State ad campaign.

Techniques

The Creative Process

I don't have a set process. Every project is unique, and I treat it that way. I just dive in and start creating, and during this time, new ideas and techniques come to life. That's my favorite part! Poser is perfect for the previsualization stage of the process when something needs to be shown to the client right away. I utilize the quick lighting setups and texture packages. I usually start with these items as a base, because it eliminates a lot of preliminary work that goes into creating believable textures and staging.

Step-by-Step Tutorial:
Creating "Unleash Your Horses"

SeventhStreet just finished the second year of print campaigns for Quaker State called "Unleash Your Horses." The project consisted of three print ads (see Figures 13.4, 13.5, and 13.6) involving a vehicle racing down a road flanked by computer-generated horses made of oil. The project was produced for Doner Detroit (Quaker State's advertising agency) with our CG partner Digital Image Studios (DIS) in Farmington Hills, Michigan. Because the final model was being worked on in Maya, I used Poser on the same day as the shoot to help the client visualize the horse placement, poses, facial expressions, and relationship to the vehicles.

1. I begin the project by using some stock horse models and applying morph targets within Poser to get them closer to the final vision. See Figures 13.1 and 13.2.

2. Now I have a horse model that I like and a background plate from the photo shoot. I use Poser to set up the scene, camera position, and horse poses. This way I can get a quick signoff from our client and move right into production. See Figure 13.3.

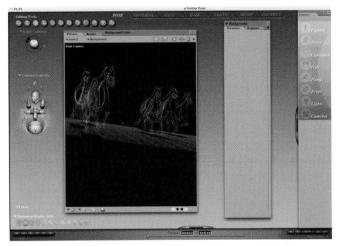

Figure 13.1 Apply morph targets to the stock horse model wireframes.

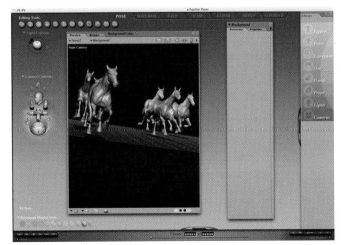

Figure 13.2 Preview the approximation of the final horse models.

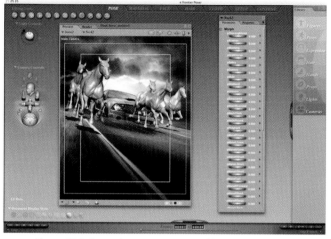

Figure 13.3 Set up the scene, camera, and horse poses in Poser.

3. From here, I use the BodyStudio (by ReissStudio) plug-in for Maya to import the Poser data, keeping all the poses and camera coordinates from the Poser file. Figures 13.4, 13.5, and 13.6 are the three finished ads.

Figure 13.4 "Unleash Your Horses" Quaker State ad campaign final image one.

Figure 13.5 "Unleash Your Horses" Quaker State ad campaign final image two.

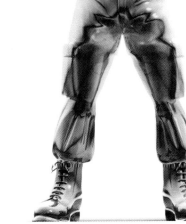

Figure 13.6 "Quaker State Oil Man."
Quaker State ad campaign final image three.

Insights

Lighting

Lighting is tricky, and it can make or break your image. Even if you have the greatest model and texture, poor lighting can kill it. Keeping it simple is always the best solution. I start with a single source light that is going to be the most flattering for my subject.. From there, I start adding some fill lighting and ambiance. Sometimes combining two different lighting techniques—such as spotlights combined with a dimmed IBL—brings about the greatest results. For instance, with a portrait, I use a directional light from one side, come in and use a subtle fill light from the opposite side, and maybe finish it with a nice hard rim light for the edges of the face.

Content

Content is crucial. It saves me a ton of time and headaches when I start with Poser stock content and third-party content and then alter it to fit my needs. I go to Renderosity.com fairly often to see what is new and "hot."

Previsualization Tool

Poser works great as a previsualization tool for people who are not familiar with the 3D world. The program's simple interface allows clients to sit over your shoulder and become involved because Poser makes it easy for them to understand how you get from wireframe to finished image.

Q&A

What are some of your timesaving tips when using Poser on a project or artwork?

I start with the pose and body shape and a simple single or double light setup. When I have the basics down, I can spend days finessing from there.

What advice do you have for artists who are starting out with Poser?

Use the provided models and texture packages to start out. They are easy one-click solutions, and you typically won't run into problems with bad polygons or misplaced texture maps. When you have the basics down, you can venture into the custom texture packages, model morphs, and lighting setups.

What are some of your favorite Poser features?

I would have to say it is the Ambient Occlusion and FireFly. Without these things, I would never be able to achieve the realism that I am looking for.

Where do you think computer-generated imagery will be 5–10 years from now?

I think the better question is, "Where will the traditional imagery be?"

Resources

On the DVD

- Artist Gallery

Links

- http://www.howdesign.com
- http://www.turbosquid.com
- http://www.creativehotlist.com
- http://www.3dcar-gallery.com
- http://www.3dcommune.com
- http://www.3dcafe.com
- http://www.modernpostcard.com
- http://www.renderosity.com
- http://www.contentparadise.com
- http://www.daz3d.com
- http://www.seventh-street.com
- http://www.dimage.com

MIKE CAMPAU

Studio

Software: Poser, Mac OS X, Photoshop, Illustrator, Maya

Hardware: Mac PowerPC G5 Dual 2GHz, dual monitors (20-inch studio displays)

Contact

Mike Campau ■ SeventhStreet Integrated Creative Services ■ Birmingham, Michigan ■ http://www.seventh-street.com

MIKE CAMPAU

ILLUSTRATION

Gallery

"African American James."

MIKE CAMPAU

"Bballin."

ILLUSTRATION

"BlueEyes."

"Real Bryn2."

"Real James."

"Blue 2."

SCOTT THIGPEN

About the Artist

Scott has never known a time that he was not drawing. Even when he was a child, he was making works of art with crayons, pens, pencils, mashed potatoes, or anything else he could get his hands on. Although Scott went to college, he did not get his degree in art, and he gained most of his skills teaching himself.

When he was in grad school, he decided to drop out and become an animator. He put together a portfolio and sent it out to more than 20 animation firms. He was rejected by every one of them. Feeling defeated, he spent the next 10 years working odd jobs and sketching in his free time.

When Scott realized that he had a talent for illustration, he spent every moment he could honing his skill. He would wake up at 4:00 each morning before work and draw as much as he could until he felt confident that he could go completely freelance. Things were hard at first; however, with time, he earned the trust of clients and landed an agent.

Scott has done work for *Modern Bride*, *The Wall Street Journal*, The American Bar Association, Snapple, Gillette, Harlequin Romance Novels, and The Chicago Bears, to name a few.

Artist's Statement

I really don't consider myself an artist in the sense of a visual artist. What really keeps me going is that I can't stand the thought of a boss. Also, when I wasn't a professional commercial illustrator, I would always sneer at the terrible art out there and how I could do better. Then a very wise illustrator shared this advice from Calvin Coolidge:

"Nothing in the world can take the place of Persistence. Talent will not; nothing is more common than unsuccessful men with talent. Genius will not; unrewarded genius is almost a proverb. Education will not; the world is full of educated derelicts. Persistence and determination alone are omnipotent. The slogan 'Press On' has solved and always will solve the problems of the human race."

After that, I learned that persistence was the key to being a good illustrator (or anything else I set my mind to).

I do consider myself an artist, because I have found that I tend to look at the world differently from most people (whether I would want to or not). To me, most things are fantasy. Tiles in floors become stepping-stones to a secret place. Textured walls become stories and pictures. I feel that is what shapes me as an artist.

Influences

Artists who have influenced my life include Kirsten Ulve and Luc Latulippe. Inspirations and influences include drudge, political corruptness, religious hypocrisy, and other Orwellian things that fuel my brain to constantly come up with creative things.

"Non-drinker."

ILLUSTRATION

Techniques

The Creative Process

I'm terribly dyslexic; however, I don't see this as a curse. My mind does not comprehend math, details, instructions, and other important issues very well. However, if you say "pink fuzzy elephant," my mind can generate some 1,000 odd images almost instantaneously from the utterance of the concept. Due to my dyslexia, I'm able to transpose the image in my head and get it just how I want it to look. By then, Poser helps solidify and verify my idea. Poser is a tool for me to take an image, pose it accordingly, and then zip the camera around all ways to get the best look for a dramatic scene.

Most of the time when I start a project, I'm already behind (due to the demand from my clients). I usually have to hit the pavement running, trying to beat the deadline. This is usually extremely frustrating and terribly hard, especially when I need to make sure I have the proportions of my artwork correct.

When I finally get in my head the certain pose I want to draw, I launch Poser and select the Ben, Jessi, or James stock Poser figure. Because the final picture for me is a 2D illustration and not a 3D image, I don't really focus on high-resolution renders or the skin surfaces. Instead, I'm mainly concerned with the pose and how accurate I can make it.

I found out that I could spend hundreds and hundreds of dollars on sites that offer preposed characters (as well as the characters themselves). To avoid that expense, I just use the stock poses that come with Poser and work from there.

There is a slight learning curve in getting your poses exactly the way you want them. However, I've found the golden rule of Save Often helps (as does Save As when you come to a point that you like a particular pose but want to try a different avenue).

Step-by-Step Tutorial: Creating the "Atlanta Rollergirls"

My work is almost always done digitally; I use a 12-inch Tablet PC to do all my sketches. When given an assignment, I usually draw a few preliminary sketches and then forward them to the client. Sometimes the client loves it. Other times I get requests for a revision. The hardest thing for me to draw is the human body (which is odd, figuring that about 99 percent of my jobs are of humans). It is challenging and at times almost impossible to get the pose I need.

Figure 14.6 is a poster I did for the Atlanta Rollergirls. They wanted one girl hitting another with a snowball in a "rough and tumble" style. My first rendition (see Figure 14.1) was not powerful enough, and it didn't really fit the bill of what they wanted. This left only one solution: Poser. I had a little wooden dummy doll that I used, but it would never bend or twist exactly the way I needed it to; fortunately, Poser gives me the power that I need.

Figure 14.1 This sketch was not powerful enough for the client.

1. I now have the ability to lay out one girl getting hit and spin the scene around until I get the best angle. I also light the figure in Poser. See Figure 14.2.

Figure 14.2 Find the best camera angle and light the figures.

2. After I finish my work in Poser, I return to my digital sketchpad and redraw the image. A lot of times I trace over the 3D image and stylize it from there. I would not be able to get this look and feel without the use of Poser. I highly recommend Poser when working on an illustration. See Figure 14.3.

Figure 14.3 Trace over the Poser image and then stylize.

3. After I finish my sketch, I open Adobe Illustrator and start the labor-intensive clicking of Bezier curves. Once I get a working proof in Adobe Illustrator, I send it to the client for feedback. This particular client has a lot of revisions. See Figure 14.4.

4. I make the requested changes, and then the picture is ready for the graphic designer to add text and lay it out for printing. See Figure 14.5.

I LOVE the "dark on light/light on dark" line work! What do you think of this dk blue/lt blue combo? I think it's less shocking and contrasty. JUST a suggestion, though.

Could you draw bangs on this girl, or something, so she looks less bald?

Figure 14.4 The client's revisions.

Figure 14.5 The picture is ready for layout.

Figure 14.6 is the final version of the "Atlanta Rollergirls" poster. (Designer Chris Thoren did all the typeface and textual layouts.)

Figure 14.6 "Atlanta Rollergirls" final poster image.

Step-by-Step Tutorial: Walking Boy

For this project, I have to draw a little boy walking home with a financial "report card." Figure 14.7 shows my drawing of the boy freehand. Two of the biggest challenges I've always had are showing weight and a person walking. Fortunately, Poser is a godsend for eliminating this particular problem.

Figure 14.7 A freehand drawing of the little boy.

1. The boy has to appear around 10 or 11 years of age, so the Poser model Ben is the perfect match. Once Ben loads, I go straight into the stock poses and select the walk. See Figure 14.8.

TIP

I have much more success making accurate tweaks if I turn Inverse Kinematics off in the Figure menu. Then I have the freedom to move the legs/feet any way I please.

ILLUSTRATION

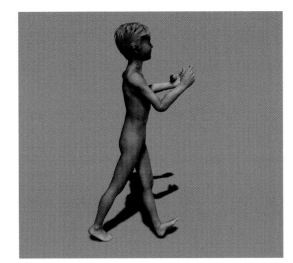

Figure 14.8 Use Ben (a stock Poser model) and apply a stock walking pose.

While I work, I am constantly shifting the camera around and zooming in and out to make sure my pose is completely accurate on all sides. (I've made the mistake many times of getting a pose I thought I liked only to find out that when I shifted the camera, the pose was completely off.) Also, I am very familiar with the great Undo tool (⌘+Z for Mac, Ctrl+Z for Windows).

Once I get the pose I want, I think about how the light is going to hit my character. I usually pick one of the stock lights and then shift the lights around until the lighting is exactly how I want it. After that, I do some quick test renders to make sure that I have everything just so.

NOTE

One of my all-time-favorite things to do in Poser is working with the hands. Since computers aren't perfect (although they would like to think they are), when I shift the hands to a grip, the fingers get messed up. It's nice that Poser allows complete control of each joint of the hand so that you can get that exact pose you want. Hands and fingers are hard enough to draw from memory, so being able to get the exact pose of the hand that I want is yet another godsend.

2. When I have the pose and lighting the way I like it, I always do a high-resolution render of my picture. In Poser, I select Render Dimensions, set them to some absurdly large size (such as 3200×3200), and set the dpi at 300. From there, I'm able to take the pose into Photoshop and alter it if needed. Then it's ready for printing to use on my light table or Tablet PC. (I generally use a Tablet PC, but I like to have the option to print if needed.)

3. Once I render my project, the rest of it is my working in Autodesk Sketchbook Pro and Adobe Illustrator. I basically just build up my project page layered upon the page while sketching. From my Poser render, I make a simple sketch, and from there, I bend the proportions accordingly. (I try to work for a highly stylized look.) Figure 14.9 is the sketch I made from the Poser render for this project.

Figure 14.9 Sketch over the Poser model printout.

Figure 14.10 After some post work in Illustrator, here is the finished image.

4. When I have my sketch completely sketched out to the detail I want, I go into Adobe Illustrator and click away until I have the picture exactly the way I want. I usually get all this done within 4–5 hours. Figure 14.10 is the ready-for-print picture of a boy that began as a 3D model in Poser and was transformed into vector artwork in Illustrator. The client was pleased with it, and so was I. Now if only Poser could take my Illustrator pictures and make them into Poser models...

Insights

Lighting

I have just started to use Poser lighting. I usually create my own light in Adobe Illustrator; however, just being able to adjust the lights on the fly is a godsend.

Posing Figures

It's always near impossible to get two people in a lovey-dovey pose to hug or clasp just right. It can be challenging getting things positioned just so. The obvious easy fix is to shift the camera around to where I can see the issue and fix it.

Q&A

What advice do you have for artists who are starting out with Poser?

You could invest in models, but by the time you've paid them to accomplish the same effect, you would be better off buying Poser.

What do you think will be most significant in CGI 5–10 years from now?

Showing the correct issue of weight and movement. I loved the *Lord of the Ring Trilogy* immensely, but anytime they got a CGI character to do a real-life person stunt, it was always noticeable that it was 3D.

What are some of your favorite Poser features?

I love the expressions and being able to use the dials on the fly. That's been the best feature for me. Other things are the "grasp" feature on the hand and the facial expressions.

Resources

On the DVD

- Artist Gallery

Links

- http://www.digg.com
- http://www.lifehacker.com
- http://www.flickr.com
- http://del.icio.us

SCOTT THIGPEN

Studio

Software: Poser, Autodesk SketchBook Pro, Adobe Illustrator

Hardware: Toshiba 14-inch Tablet PC with 1GB of RAM

Contact

Scott Thigpen ■ Auburn, Alabama ■ scott@sthig.com ■ http://www.sthig.com

Gallery

"Ali."

"Elaine High Tower."

"Horoscope."

"Nice Buns."

"Marla."

"Dominatrix."

"Yacht."

a Harders ©2005 www.mec4d.com Poser6

CATHARINA HARDERS

About the Artist

Catharina Harders is a graduate of visual arts, design, color, and the human form. Her understanding and use of technology, along with her understanding of photography and light and 11years' experience with modeling/TV/film work, allow her to display her artistic talent, giving her artwork a definitive presence. She is highly recognized within the 3D community and has acquired a reputation as one of the best creators of digital character and UV texture maps. Her photo-realistic textures have become best sellers on the Internet, and she attributes much of this success to her mastery of Poser, Deep Paint, and Deep UV. Much of Catharina's work reflects a distinct originality and is unique in its ability to evoke emotion. As such, Catharina has won many awards. Her characters portray a high standard of realism, and her work is considered revolutionary in character believability.

Artist's Statement

I have a passion for and have followed many traditional kinds of artwork; however, my greatest love lies in the creation of digital computer graphics. Poser allows me to reach the goal I have and to push my creativity to the limit. Today, I can't think of working without Poser. I use it to do just about everything, from magazine covers to virtual scenes blended into real video scenes. Poser is simple but powerful software if you know how to use it and have a good eye and attention to detail. I've spent many hours working with Poser and have learned from both my bad and good experiences. Today I am in a position of power with it.

Influences

I started working with graphics in 1995, retouching damaged digital photos for a laboratory. It was always so interesting to see all the faces, and I had an idea about how to create a digital human. This idea excited me and gave me inspiration. I started searching the Internet for all information regarding 3D human modeling.

The first artist I found (who later became my good friend and master) was Steven Stahlberg. He got me started using Maya and gave me so much inspiration and motivation that art turned into passion for me. Steven helped me and always gave me good feedback regarding my work. A short while later, I found the wonderful work of Martin Murphy. I contacted Martin, and he gave me many tips about the lil' Poser world of that time.

I started to visit the online community and share my experiences with Poser. We were all green at that time, and we didn't have anybody or anything to help us. So we learned Poser from the beginning, step by step. New features in Poser allow our work to get better and better.

I've spent the last years of my life working with many kinds of art, but I notice that every time I make something, my Poser screen is open again and again. I just can't make art without it anymore. I love to work alone, just me and my art. I don't like automatic things where you just push the button. That doesn't give me inspiration in my artwork. I don't follow other artists. I always create my own way of working. I love to read about new techniques, but I never use it for my work. I love to be original and unique. That's why all the work I've created in the past few years is unique. It's based on my own ideas, tips, and inspirations. It is just my art.

"Run Froger."

PHOTO-REALISM

Techniques

The Creative Process

I've learned many new things, but I always start with a good idea—usually something I've never tried before. Trying to do something that nobody else has done excites me, and sometimes I spend many hours, day after day, testing my techniques. After that, I start the process again and discover even more new things to keep myself curious. I use Poser not only for creating realistic images but also for creating video clips that mix reality and the virtual world. Poser is fast, and the effects I get amaze the clients.

Step-by-Step Tutorial: Creating Virtual Light Probe Angular Maps to Use with Poser IBL

Image-based lighting (IBL) is a powerful lighting feature in Poser. It's a light that illuminates the scene by recording all light information into an image map. It allows me to create wonderful virtual reality light scenes using one simple light. Light is an important—if not *the* most important—element in visual art. The following technique that I use in my renders brings the best of the IBL feature and sets my scenes in a new light and dimension. A *light probe* is incomparable for lighting a high-dynamic range 360-degree panoramic image. I use it both to light objects and as a specular texture map for shiny objects in the scene. For this technique, I'm using the following software:

- Adobe Photoshop
- HDR Shop (High Dynamic Range [HDR] image processing and manipulation software available from http://www.hdrshop.com)
- Poser

> **NOTE**
>
> *Image-based lighting* (IBL) in Poser and other 3D applications uses a special type of image known as a light probe. A *light probe* provides the image data with which to light the scene. It is a 360-degree light distribution contained in a map, which is typically created with digital cameras and reflective spheres. The gazing balls that are available from garden stores provide high-quality light-probe images.

1. First, I create a new image document in Photoshop that is 1000 pixels wide and 500 pixels high. This is the Latitude-Longitude image that I use for the base of my custom IBL and light probe. The aspect ratio for the Latitude-Longitude image is always 2:1.

2. Next, I create another new image document that is 1000 pixels wide and 250 pixels high. I use this image for the light probe. In Poser, this is the area where the light comes from the scene above the ground when using the IBL.

3. Then I choose a round brush with white color and paint on the second image I just created. The left and right sides of the images are actually the back sides of the light probe, so if I paint a white point here, simulating a spotlight, it lights the scene from behind. See Figure 15.1 for an illustration of how the light probe works in Poser IBL.

4. For the next step, I paint the light using different colors. I also use the Blur filter to get more of a soft light effect without hard edges. See Figure 15.2. Now I am done with the Latitude-Longitude map and ready for the next step.

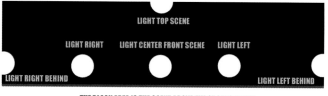

Figure 15.1 Latitude-Longitude image map at 1000×500 pixels.

Figure 15.2 The finished virtual Latitude-Longitude image map; the color points represent the spotlights.

5. I open HDR Shop and the Latitude-Longitude image map I just created in Photoshop. I okay the window that opens and says, "Specify Camera Response Curve for LDR Image." Then, in the menu bar, I choose Select, Image, Panorama, Panoramic Transformations.

In the Panoramic Transform window, I select Latitude-Longitude as the Source Image format, with Width set at 1000 and Height set at 500. I set 3D Rotation to None. For the Destination Image, I select Light Probe (Angular Map) as the format, with Width and Height both set at 1024. I use 1:1 for Aspect Ratio and then click OK. See Figure 15.3 for a screenshot of these settings.

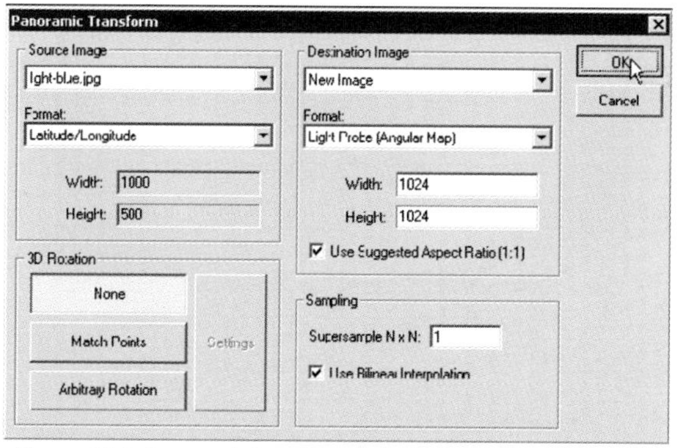

Figure 15.3 Panoramic Transform dialog box settings in HDR Shop.

6. In Figure 15.4, I have created my own virtual light probe image map that I can use in Poser and plug into IBL. I choose Save Image as Low Dynamic Range (LDR) Image JPEG so that I can use it with Poser 6, because only Poser 7 supports high dynamic range images (HDRI).

TIP

The light probe in Figure 15.4 is only an example. If you are going to create your own light probe, remember to paint your lights on a black image map. That way, everything other than black will create light in your scene.

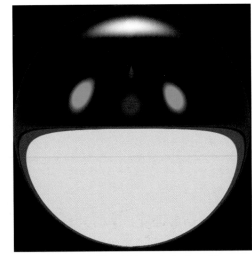

Figure 15.4 Virtual light probe for Poser IBL.

7. These last two steps show how I set the IBL in Poser and how it works. It should provide a better understanding of the way light probes work under IBL.

In Poser, I put a ball prop (or any other object) into the scene, remove all default lights from the scene, and then create a new light. I double-click on the light, and in the light Properties, I check the boxes Diffuse IBL and Ambient Occlusion (AO). I then click the Scene AO Options button. I set the Max Distance to 5.999532, the Bias to 0.049846, and Num Samples to 3. These settings are important but also optional. AO does give more reality to the scenes.

8. In the Material room, I load the light probe image that I just created into the color of the light. I set Intensity to Max 1.000000; the best is 0.658505. I set Image Resolution to 1024 and IBL Contrast to 0.010000. Then I return to the Pose room.

I click the Render button and see the excellent work of this custom light probe. The scene is now lit up with only a simple IBL AO light but is using a real light probe. I do not recommend using mirrored images. When I use IBL AO, it is important that the quality of the render is good. I use the Auto Setting and set the slider all the way to the right or at least to Final. It increases rendering time, but I get a higher quality render, especially with high-resolution images.

> ## TIP
>
> For more realistic reflections, use a photo of a light probe. To do that, you need to buy a silver ball. Then you can import the photo directly into the IBL.

Creating Photo-Realistic Reflections: Samples

Reflections are one of the most important things when rendering Poser photo-realism scenes. Everything in the real world reflects in some way, thanks to the fact that our eyes can catch and recognize the depth of the object and the surface.

New Poser features allow us to create almost any reflection that we can imagine. With the new IBL features, we can really push our creativity to the limits. The screen shots that follow show several simple examples of reflecting surfaces and the settings in the Material room that I use in almost in every render I create, from a mirrored silver ball to the eyes or the self.

The scene can't be empty, because objects need to reflect something. If we put a ball with reflection node on the ground, it does not give the expected effect. Think about a mirror in an empty room; it only reflects the empty room.

Figures 15.5 through 15.14 show the settings I use in the Material room to create different kinds of reflections. Simple materials can give the illusion of reality in Poser renders and really fool the viewer's eyes.

Figure 15.5 Virtual reality in Poser.

Figure 15.6 The most commonly used reflection in my renders is a 100 percent mirror reflection. This reflection can also be used as a chrome metal reflection and is known as *specular reflection*.

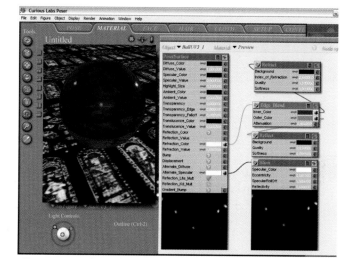

Figure 15.7 A glass with reflection. You can change the color or just use pure glass. Here, I also used custom specular maps for the light reflection.

Figure 15.8 A half-matte plastic, silicon surface.

PHOTO-REALISM

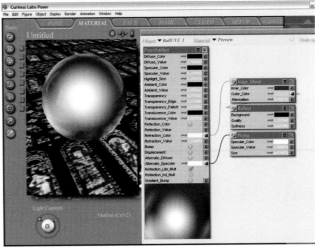

Figure 15.9 A setting to use, for example, on a car surface. It's a high-reflection surface.

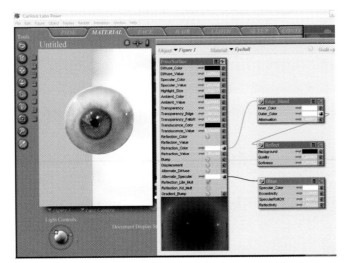

Figure 15.11 A glass reflection used for the eyeballs' surfaces and tiny glass surfaces.

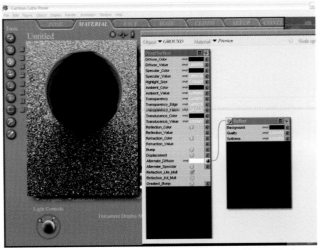

Figure 15.10 A black surface with soft reflection, used for polished stones and all types of dark surfaces.

Figure 15.12 Image rendered using Poser, with new features as IBL, AO, and reflections.

Figure 15.13 Here, I used a couple different materials. For the floor, I used the 100 percent mirror reflection settings shown in Figure 15.6. For the car surface, I used the high-reflection settings shown in Figure 15.9 and changed the diffuse color to red.

Figure 15.14 Here, I used the setting from all the materials presented in Figures 15.4 through 15.13.

TIP

The key for creating convincing photo-reality in Poser is remembering that the effect is driven by reflection, light, and shadow. (And don't forget that for the best rendering quality, you need to render all your scenes on the Final setting.)

Insights

Lighting

A good light is so important. My step-by-step technique shows a way to create IBL by using HDR Shop to create original Poser light probes that reflect light in my scenes the way it works in reality. It is a simple process, but it takes a good amount of time and materials to get what I need before I can start with a professional scene. Poser 7 supports high dynamic range imaging (HDRI), but even low dynamic range imaging (LDRI) in Poser 6 is enough to fool the eyes of the viewers. IBL is powerful and fast; I use it for all my scenes no matter how simple the scene is. It's a must for the base scene because I am trying to create for virtual reality. I expect to see photo-realistic images at the end of my processes working with Poser.

CATHARINA HARDERS

257

Content

For me, stock content isn't really that important. I use it from time to time, but I love to create my own art and to use my own elements in my scenes. I always take all the time I need, no matter how long it takes.

Q&A

What advice do you have for artists who are starting out with Poser?

The first thing I will say is go and read the manual! Most new users see my art and want to jump to the next level and forget about the basics they need to know. Before they can understand what I'm talking about, they need to learn the basics and understand how the software works. It's important to learn the terminology and start with the simple things to better understand the work of Poser. The Poser community usually welcomes and helps new users with any problems.

Where do you think computer-generated imagery will be 5–10 years from now?

When I see what has happened in the past eight years, I am amazed at how fast it is going. I believe in the next 10 years, we will able to generate virtual reality with just a click of the mouse. It may not be art anymore, but it will still be exciting. The human form has always been the most interesting for the CGI artists. Everything is leading up to the era of virtual humans, but for now we are still missing something. I believe that in about 10 years, we will find the answers for all our questions. Today, we can create everything we can imagine (besides the human form), but it doesn't always look real.

What are some of your favorite Poser features?

I love them all, but my favorite features are IBL and AO. I've spent so many months on this theme, testing everything until I was happy with it. These are the two features that take up most of my time while I am working on my scenes.

Resources

On the DVD

- Animation: "Beetlejuice"
- Animation: Demo-reel
- Animation: "The Day of the Dragon"
- Animation: "Woody" by Anubis
- Animation: "Worm, Apple"
- Animation: "The Forest Park"

Links

- http://forums.cgsociety.org/
- http://www.renderosity.com

CATHARINA HARDERS

Studio

Software: Poser, Photoshop, After Effects, Particle Illusion, Cinema 4D, Vue, and many others

Hardware: Pentium 4 CPU with 3.1GHz, graphic card Radeon 9700 Pro, Windows XP

Contact

Catharina Harders ■ Mec4D ■ Harlingen, The Netherlands ■ sales@mec4d.com ■ http://www.mec4d.com

Gallery

Poser 6 Revealed: The Official Guide. Original cover image.

CATHARINA HARDERS

PHOTO-REALISM

"The Day of the Dragon." Poser render.

"Egypt." 2D-3D Integration Poser 3D Balls.

PHOTO-REALISM

"Lemons." Poser AO IBL 3D render.

"The End of Tomorrow." Poser AO IBL 3D render.

CATHARINA HARDERS

PHOTO-REALISM

"The Forest Twins." Poser AO IBL 3D render.

"Eggs." Poser AO IBL 3D render.

CATHARINA HARDERS

PHOTO-REALISM

The LATCH WORM Poser6 SSS|T Render By Catharina Harders ©2005 www.mec4d.com

"The Latch Worm." Poser SSST.

Poser6 Rendering By Catharina Harders ©2005 www.mec4d.com

"2 Worms." Poser.

PHOTO-REALISM

"Help—I Need Help!" Poser AO IBL Studio Light render.

Broken legs By Catharina Harders ©2005 www.mec4d.com Poser6

"Broken Legs." Poser render.

FABRICE DELAGE (c)

FABRICE DELAGE

About the Artist

Fabrice Delage is a dedicated French graphic artist who takes photo-realism to a whole new level and continues to awe people with his lifelike Poser images. He is a self-taught designer whose high artistic standards are recognized by his peers. Fabrice is also a Runtime DNA featured artist.

Artist's Statement

I love making portraits, but I want them to look real. I want to give life to my characters by giving them the right skin texture, the right glow, the right hair wave pattern, and so on. Every detail counts. By toying around with the available technology, I feel I am on my way toward achieving my quest for digital realism.

Influences

My love of portraits and quest for realism are my true motivations. I had to wait for the technology to be available to create what I was looking for and to become a full-time graphic designer. Four years ago, Poser 5 gave me the tools to achieve my quest for realistic portraits.

Koji Yamagami had and still has a tremendous influence on my work. He's exceptional at making portraits that reveal the pureness and perfection of Asian features. I developed an attraction to models such as Miki, who I would consider my muse. You can see her in the Gallery at the end of this chapter.

"Maman."

Techniques

The Creative Process

I like to look at all types of magazines—from hair salon magazines to fashion magazines to knitting magazines—because they offer great examples of lighting and posing. They show different ways of capturing a face: the way the light reflects on the skin or hair, the expression, the makeup, the pose—basically what makes people real. I then challenge myself to re-create that look digitally.

I use Poser for setup, pose, and expression. A big part of my creative process is post work. I do a lot of work on the hair, skin, and makeup because I like texture. I don't do much on the background. Painting also plays a role in my creative process. Portrait making is my passion and what keeps me going. I don't work with clients yet.

Step-by-Step Tutorial: Creating Realistic Skin Texture

I like texture. In both the digital realm and in painting, my goal is to have as much texture as possible to achieve an organic and realistic portrait. For me, everything happens in the Pose room. I don't have a specific technique except for using my tools (software mostly) to their maximum capacity until I get it right. It's mostly an intuitive and time-consuming process.

I use the following process to acquire and create realistic skin textures:

1. First, I take pictures of my friends' and family members' skin without makeup. The pictures are digital (TIFF) and set on a high-contrast color scheme.

2. I cut and paste in Photoshop to align facial features like eyes, nose, and mouth with a 3D template. The template is a 2D mesh of the face in this case, created in a program such as UVMapper.

3. I use Photoshop to add make-up and touch up the skin. I usually remove elements like freckles because I am working essentially with Asian faces that don't have them. Figure 16.1 shows the result of applying real photos to the template.

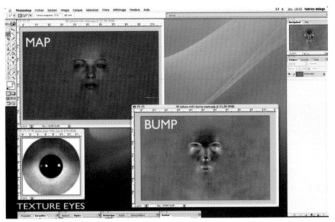

Figure 16.1 Apply real photos to a 3D template in Photoshop.

4. In Figure 16.2, I load the texture map image that I created in Photoshop into the Material room and use it as the image source channel in an Image Map node.

5. Then I touch up the lips and eyes in Poser by using a lighting scheme that simulates the particular effect I want to achieve. For the lights, I usually use the three default lights that load in Poser. I also use Outdoor, the spotlight-based portrait/figure lighting from Traveler, a Runtime DNA vendor.

6. I create test renders of my figure using the highest quality settings. Then I save the Poser scene and import it into Vue Esprit to produce more lighting effects.

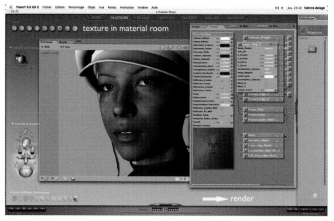

Figure 16.2 Add the texture map to the Image Map node in the Material room.

TIP

I always use the preset render settings set to the highest quality (all the way to the right). Doing that does increase the render time to painful lengths, but I find the results worth it.

7. Because I am using Poser 6, and Poser 7 is the first version of the program to support high dynamic range imaging (HDRI), I am using Vue Esprit to do the image-based lighting instead of Poser. I set the shader on a blue glow to accurately represent the lighting and shade intensity. I use the Bump channel more than displacement. I always have raytracing on because it produces a natural light.

8. Again, I render the character at the highest quality preset settings and open it back in Photoshop to do the personal work of retouching and post work. Here I create a depth of field effect and do final touch-up of skin and make-up. Figure 16.3, "Remember China," shows a final version of the model.

TIP

It takes a lot of time to give life to a face. For photo-realism, give yourself at least 24 hours. The secret in making virtual skin seem real is all about light and texture. Light does not just bounce from the skin; it glows from within, giving texture its own dimension. When you create an image that allows people to forget that it is digital, then you know you've made a realistic portrait.

Figure 16.3 "Remember China" final image.

TIP

Postproduction is as important as production. Software such as Photoshop is complementary with Poser. You have to follow your instincts to create something that looks good.

Insights

Lighting

Good lighting makes a scene real. Realism is precisely what I am after and why I spend so much time looking for the perfect lighting. I never use the templates. I just toy around with the existing tools to find the perfect light. I prefer to use Vue Esprit for image-based lighting because, prior to Poser 7, only low dynamic range images were supported. I use the Poser lighting in addition to light sets from online vendors.

Content

My favorite model, Miki, is from e frontier and Posermatic. Some of my favorite third-party content creators are ADDY (for hair painting), As Shanim (for fantasy clothes), Posermatic (for the Miki figure), and Stefyzz (for head and body texture maps). In addition, because Poser comes with hundreds of megabytes of content—including figures, clothing, hair, and other props—there is plenty of great content to choose from.

Q&A

What advice do you have for artists who are starting out with Poser?

Take time exploring the different rooms and getting to know the software. Don't limit yourself to the templates. Toy around, and give life to your model. My best tips to save time with Poser are to read the manual, understand the program, and then use Poser to its full potential. There are no shortcuts. Have fun.

What is the biggest challenge you face while using Poser?

I have one main challenge while using Poser: the structure of the directory. Because I am using the localized French version of Poser, the library contents are not ordered in my language's alphabetical order; instead, they are ordered based on their original English alphabetization. This isn't really a problem, but it makes things more complicated. I've resolved this issue by creating subfolders to organize my library so that I don't have one large disorganized list.

What are the hardest postures, gestures, and expressions to create and why? Describe your process in posing your figures.

The figure definitely comes first for me. I spend a lot of time in the Pose room and with Render settings. First I work on posing the figure and the lighting, and then I tackle the scene. Expressions are difficult to create. Generating complex facial expressions from a 3D face model is hard. Several hundred parameter adjustments are necessary to precisely control the face. Such complexity is the challenge I create for myself.

I spend a lot of time adjusting the settings to make expressions as real as possible. The settings I spend most of my time adjusting are the Morph and Transform parameters in the Pose room (especially the eyes, shape of the face, cheeks). I spend at least 45 minutes adjusting each one.

Resources

On the DVD

- Artist Gallery

Links

- http://www.renderosity.com
- http://www.3dvf.com
- http://www.runtimedna.com

FABRICE DELAGE

Studio

Software: Poser, Vue Esprit, Photoshop, ZBrush, Vue 5 Infinite

Hardware: Power Macintosh G5, Power Macintosh G4, eBook graphics tablet

Contact

Fabrice Delage ■ Destyling Form ■ Lieusaint, France ■ fabrice.delage@club-internet.fr

PHOTO-REALISM

CHAPTER 16

Gallery

"BVH."

"Cho."

276

"Linda."

"Miki."

FABRICE DELAGE

PHOTO-REALISM

"Tam."

"Uzil."

alpha channel—An 8-bit layer in a graphics file format that is used to express transparency.

ambient color—A global pervasive light color that is applied to the entire scene.

ambient occlusion (AO)—An effect that diminishes ambient light from the scene based on surrounding geometry, thus causing shadows to appear more realistic within the scene context. The soft appearance achieved by ambient occlusion alone is similar to the way an object appears on an overcast day.

antialiasing—A process of smoothing rendered edges to remove jagged edges.

background image—An image that is set to appear behind the scene.

body part—Any one of the defined pieces that make up a figure.

body part group—Polygons that share the same name as the bone that is controlling them.

bone—An invisible object that exists beneath the surface of the figure and defines the way the attached body part moves as the bone moves.

Bone Creation tool—A tool used to create and place new bones.

bulge—The process of increasing a muscle's size as a joint's angle is decreased.

bump map—A 2D bitmap image that adds a relief texture to the surface of an object—like the surface of an orange rind.

Camera Dots—An interface control used to remember and recall camera position and properties.

Chain Break tool—A tool used to prevent the movement of one object from moving a connected object from its current position.

child—The following object in a hierarchy chain. Child objects move in conjunction with the parent object but can move independently as well.

cloth simulation—The process of calculating the position and deformation of a cloth object as it is moved by forces and collides with various scene objects.

clothify—The process of converting a prop object into a cloth object.

collision—An event that occurs when a vertex of a cloth object intersects with the polygon face of a scene object.

compiled file—A Python file that has been converted to a machine-savvy format that is no longer readable text but that executes more quickly.

conforming clothes—Clothes or props that are designed to fit the given character exactly and to remain fitting as the figure's pose changes.

conforming prop—An object that is deformed to fit the designated figure.

damping—The tendency of an object to resist bouncing after it is set in motion. The opposite of springiness.

deformer—An object used to deform the surface of body parts by moving vertices.

depth cueing—An atmospheric effect that makes objects farther in the scene appear hazier.

depth map shadows—Shadows that are calculated, with the shadow information saved in a 2D grayscale map, resulting in shadows with soft edges.

diffuse color—The surface color of an object.

displacement map—A 2D bitmap image that controls the displacement of geometry objects.

display ports—Additional sections of the Document window that can display a different view of the scene.

display styles—Render options for the Document window.

Document window—The main window interface where the posed figure is displayed.

draping—The process of letting a cloth object fall to rest about a scene object.

dynamics—The branch of physics that is concerned with the effects of forces on the motion of objects.

editing tools—A selection of tools used to manipulate and transform scene elements.

element—Any scene object that can be selected, including body parts, props, cameras, and lights.

exporting—The process of saving Poser files to a format to be used by another program.

expression—Facial features saved in a unique position to show different emotions.

face shape—The underlying 3D geometry on which the texture is mapped to create the face.

face texture map—An image that is wrapped about the head model to show details.

figure—A character loaded into Poser that can be posed using the various interface controls.

Figure Circle control—A circle that surrounds the figure and enables it to be moved as one unit.

FireFly render engine—The default rendering method for rendering images in Poser. This engine includes many advanced features such as raytracing, 3D motion blur, displacement, and texture filtering.

Flash—A vector-based format commonly used to display images and movies on the Web.

Floating control—An interface object that isn't attached to the interface window and can be placed anywhere within that window.

focal length—A camera property that changes the center focus point for the camera.

frame rate—The rate at which frames of an animation sequence are displayed. Higher frame rates result in smoother motion but require more memory.

guide hairs—A sampling of hairs that show where the full set of hair will be located and how it will be shaped.

Gaussian blur—A widely used effect in graphics software such as Adobe Photoshop, The GIMP, and Paint.NET. It is typically used to reduce image noise and detail levels.

hair density—The total number of hairs for a given hair group.

hair growth group—A grouped selection of polygons that define where the hair is to be located.

hair root—The end of the hair nearest the figure.

Hair Style tool—A tool that is used to style individual hairs or groups of selected hairs.

hair tip—The end of the hair farthest away from the figure.

HDRI—In computer graphics and cinematography, high dynamic range imaging is a set of techniques that allow a far greater dynamic range of exposures (that is, a large difference between light and dark areas) than normal digital imaging techniques.

hierarchy—A linked chain of objects connected from parent to child.

highlight—The spot on an object where the light is reflected with the greatest intensity. Also known as a *specular* highlight.

IK chain—A set of hierarchically linked bones that are enabled using Inverse Kinematics, including root and goal objects.

image-based lighting (IBL)—Lighting that illuminates the scene by recording all light information into an image map.

importing—The process of loading externally created files into Poser.

inclusion and exclusion angles—Angles used to mark the polygons that are affected and unaffected by the joint's movement.

infinite light—A light that simulates shining from an infinite distance so that all light rays are parallel.

interface—A set of controls used to interact with the software features.

interpolation—A calculation process used to determine the intermediate position of objects between two keyframes.

Inverse Kinematics—A unique method of calculating the motion of linked objects that enables child objects to control the position and orientation of their parent object.

joint—The base of a bone that marks the position between two bones where the body parts bend.

keyframe—A defined state of an object at one point during an animation sequence that is used to interpolate motion.

kinematics—The branch of physics that is used to calculate the movement of linked objects.

library—A collection of data that can be loaded into the scene.

locked prop—A locked prop is one whose position and orientation are set and cannot be changed unless the object is unlocked.

loop—A setting that causes an animation to repeat indefinitely.

mask—A pattern used to transfer a design onto an object.

Material group—A group of selected polygons that define a region where similar materials, such as a shirt or pants group, are applied.

Material node—A palette of material properties that can be connected to control another material value.

Morph target—A custom parameter that defines an object deformation that appears as a parameter in the Parameters palette.

Morphing tool—A tool used to sculpt the shape of a face.

Motion blur—A rendering option that blurs objects moving quickly in the scene.

motion capture—A process of collecting motion data using a special sensor that is attached to people who are performing the action.

normal—A nonrendered vector that extends from the center of each polygon face and indicates the direction that the polygon face is pointing.

NURBS—Short for non-uniform, rational B-spline, it is a mathematical model commonly used in computer graphics for generating and representing curves and surfaces.

offset—The location of an imported prop as measured from the scene's origin point.

opacity—The property that makes objects appear solid. The opposite of *transparency.*

OpenGL—An industry standard graphics specification that enables hardware acceleration for fast Document window updates when used with supporting hardware.

orphan polygons—Polygons that don't belong to a group.

parent—The controlling object that a child object is attached to. When the parent moves, the child object moves with it.

phonemes—Facial expressions that occur when different speaking sounds are made.

Pin tool—A tool that prevents vertices from moving out of position.

point light—A light that projects light rays in all directions equally.

Pose Dots—An interface control used to remember a specific figure pose.

PoserPython—An extension of the industry-standard Python scripting language that allows users to extend and add new functionality to Poser.

Preferences—An interface for setting defaults and for configuring the interface.

prop—Any external object added to the scene to enhance the final image. Props may include scenery, figure accessories, clothes, and hair.

Python—An interpreted, object-oriented scripting language that includes text commands for defining certain actions.

Python Scripts palette—An interface where you can load and execute Python scripts.

raytrace shadows—Shadows that are calculated using an accurate raytracing method that results in sharp edges.

raytracing—A rendering method that calculates the scene by casting light rays into the scene and following these light rays as they bounce off objects. The results are accurately rendered shadows, reflections, and materials.

render—The process of calculating the final look of all scene geometries, lights, materials, and textures into a final image.

render farm—Also termed a render wall, this is a computer cluster to render computer-generated imagery (CGI), typically for film and television visual effects.

room tabs—A set of tabs located at the top of the Poser interface that allow access to various feature interfaces.

Root node—The top-level material node; also called the PoserSurface node.

rotation—The process of spinning and reorienting an object within the scene.

scaling—The process of changing the size of an object within the scene.

sellion—That part of the nose that extends from its tip up between the eyes.

Shader window—An interface found in the Material room where new custom materials can be created.

shadow camera—A camera that is positioned in the same location as a light.

Side window control—A simple control positioned on the side of the interface that opens another set of controls.

simulation range—The number of frames that are included in the simulation marked by Start and End Frames.

skeleton—A hierarchy of bones arranged to match the figure it controls.

Sketch Designer—An interface that defines brushstrokes that are used to render a scene using the Sketch render engine.

source file—An original text-based Python file that can be executed.

spotlight—A light that projects light within a cone of influence.

symmetry—A property that occurs when one-half of an object is identical to the opposite side.

tapering—A scaling operation that changes the size of only one end of an object.

texture filtering—A process applied to 2D images to soften them and eliminate any jagged edges.

texture map—A 2D image file that is wrapped about a surface.

textured light—A light that projects a texture map onto the scene.

Tracking mode—Modes that define the detail of the objects displayed in the Document window.

translation—The process of moving an object within the scene.

trans map—A 2D grayscale image that determines the transparency of objects.

transparency—A material property that defines how easy an object can be seen through.

UI Dots—Interface controls that remembers a specific interface configuration.

volume effect—An atmospheric effect that colors all scene objects with the designated color, much like fog.

wacro—A custom PoserPython script used within the Shader window to create new material types.

walk cycle—A repeating set of frames that animate a figure walking.

waveform—A visual display of a sound showing its volume per time.

weld—An import option that combines vertices that have the same coordinates.

THOMSON

Create amazing 3D graphics with Poser 7 with coverage for every user, from every angle!

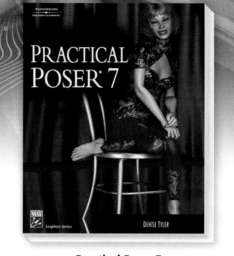

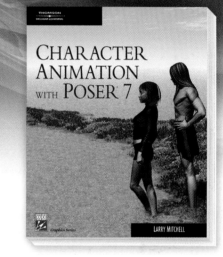

Poser 7 Revealed: The Official Guide
ISBN: 1-59863-296-5 ■ $29.99 U.S. ■ 600 pages
Level: Beginner–Intermediate

Now Poser beginners can get a thorough introduction to Poser as they learn how to use the latest version. This ideal beginner's guide uses conceptual discussions and elementary, engaging tutorials to explain each topic. Numerous hands-on tutorials cover the technical and artistic aspects of each amazing feature of Poser 7. Examine the concept behind each task by studying examples and learning the steps necessary to complete each one through comprehensive, step-by-step lessons.

Practical Poser 7
ISBN: 1-58450-478-1 ■ $49.95 U.S. ■ 540 pages ■ CD Included
Level: Intermediate–Advanced

This tutorial-style guide includes hands-on, real-world projects for using the many features of Poser. Intermediate to advanced-level Poser users will develop the skills they need to produce professional, commercial-quality work. This latest edition includes detailed coverage of animation and rendering developments in Poser 7, as well as Poser scene creation, adding realism to Poser characters, and making Poser clothing.

Character Animation with Poser 7
ISBN: 1-58450-517-6 ■ $49.95 U.S. ■ 500 pages ■ DVD Included
Level: Intermediate–Advanced

Now animators, comic artists, web designers, and game developers can easily learn the fundamentals of character animation with Poser 7. Intermediate to advanced-level users will learn how to animate characters by integrating Poser's improved workflow, better posing, lighting and rendering tools, and the all new lip synching feature for making 3D characters talk and sing. This book focuses on teaching high-quality character animation creation based on a Poser-centric integrated software workflow.

THOMSON
COURSE TECHNOLOGY
Professional ■ Technical ■ Reference

CHARLES RIVER MEDIA

Call 1.800.648.7450 to order
Order online at www.courseptr.com

License Agreement/Notice of Limited Warranty

By opening the sealed disc container in this book, you agree to the following terms and conditions. If, upon reading the following license agreement and notice of limited warranty, you cannot agree to the terms and conditions set forth, return the unused book with unopened disc to the place where you purchased it for a refund.

License

The enclosed software is copyrighted by the copyright holder(s) indicated on the software disc. You are licensed to copy the software onto a single computer for use by a single user and to a backup disc. You may not reproduce, make copies, or distribute copies or rent or lease the software in whole or in part, except with written permission of the copyright holder(s). You may transfer the enclosed disc only together with this license, and only if you destroy all other copies of the software and the transferee agrees to the terms of the license. You may not decompile, reverse assemble, or reverse engineer the software.

Notice of Limited Warranty

The enclosed disc is warranted by Thomson Course Technology PTR to be free of physical defects in materials and workmanship for a period of sixty (60) days from end user's purchase of the book/disc combination. During the sixty-day term of the limited warranty, Thomson Course Technology PTR will provide a replacement disc upon the return of a defective disc.

Limited Liability

THE SOLE REMEDY FOR BREACH OF THIS LIMITED WARRANTY SHALL CONSIST ENTIRELY OF REPLACEMENT OF THE DEFECTIVE DISC. IN NO EVENT SHALL THOMSON COURSE TECHNOLOGY PTR OR THE AUTHOR BE LIABLE FOR ANY OTHER DAMAGES, INCLUDING LOSS OR CORRUPTION OF DATA, CHANGES IN THE FUNCTIONAL CHARACTERISTICS OF THE HARDWARE OR OPERATING SYSTEM, DELETERIOUS INTERACTION WITH OTHER SOFTWARE, OR ANY OTHER SPECIAL, INCIDENTAL, OR CONSEQUENTIAL DAMAGES THAT MAY ARISE, EVEN IF THOMSON COURSE TECHNOLOGY PTR AND/OR THE AUTHOR HAS PREVIOUSLY BEEN NOTIFIED THAT THE POSSIBILITY OF SUCH DAMAGES EXISTS.

Disclaimer of Warranties

THOMSON COURSE TECHNOLOGY PTR AND THE AUTHOR SPECIFICALLY DISCLAIM ANY AND ALL OTHER WARRANTIES, EITHER EXPRESS OR IMPLIED, INCLUDING WARRANTIES OF MERCHANTABILITY, SUITABILITY TO A PARTICULAR TASK OR PURPOSE, OR FREEDOM FROM ERRORS. SOME STATES DO NOT ALLOW FOR EXCLUSION OF IMPLIED WARRANTIES OR LIMITATION OF INCIDENTAL OR CONSEQUENTIAL DAMAGES, SO THESE LIMITATIONS MIGHT NOT APPLY TO YOU.

Other

This Agreement is governed by the laws of the State of Massachusetts without regard to choice of law principles. The United Convention of Contracts for the International Sale of Goods is specifically disclaimed. This Agreement constitutes the entire agreement between you and Thomson Course Technology PTR regarding use of the software.